A Beautiful

SECOND ACT

"¡Sensasional! Get ready to be challenged with humor, insight, and grace. In her latest book, *A Beautiful Second Act*, Maria Morera Johnson presents another formidable collection of holy women whose lives remind us that we are all called to holiness, our fundamental vocation. In her trademark personal writing style, Johnson beautifully blends literature, memoir, and spiritual biography as she introduces us to her posse of saints and inspiring women—and nobody does this better!"

María Ruiz Scaperlanda
Catholic author, blogger, and journalist

"Thank God for second acts, and I mean that sincerely and prayerfully! In *A Beautiful Second Act*, Maria Morera Johnson movingly shares inspirational stories of her own transitions and those of women religious, mothers, scientists, teachers, actors, writers, activists, and more. Her wisdom is certain to help readers find the faith to surrender to God's plan for us in every act of life regardless of how daunting that plan may seem."

Melanie Rigney
Author of *Radical Saints: 21 Women for the 21st Century*

"Whether you are anxiously anticipating your 'second act' or are firmly ensconced in living it, let Maria Morera Johnson be your companion in more fully engaging with your truest God-given purpose. *A Beautiful Second Act* offers a cast of amazing women who shine their lights and point the way to living with greater momentum, desire, and soul. This is the book I wish I'd had years ago. It will be my new go-to gift for all the women in my life!"

Lisa M. Hendey
Author of *The Grace of Yes*

"With an inviting wit and a clever gift for making obscure facts entertaining, Maria Morera Johnson masterfully introduces us to something we all need—sound advice from women who have gone before us and lived lives of heroic virtue. Engaging stories build a personal and practical relationship between the reader and a variety of unique saints and soul sisters who have embraced the changes that accompany each season in life. This book has something for every woman no matter where she is on her physical or spiritual journey! A must-read for any woman who desires to age with wisdom, beauty, and amazing grace."

Kelly Wahlquist
Founder of WINE: Women In the New Evangelization

A Beautiful

SECOND ACT

Saints and Soul Sisters
Who Taught Me to ~~Be a Badass~~

Age with Grace

MARIA MORERA JOHNSON

Ave Maria Press AVE Notre Dame, Indiana

© 2025 by Maria Morera Johnson

All rights reserved. No part of this book may be used or reproduced in any manner whatsoever, except in the case of reprints in the context of reviews, without written permission from Ave Maria Press®, Inc., P.O. Box 428, Notre Dame, IN 46556, 1-800-282-1865.

Founded in 1865, Ave Maria Press is a ministry of the United States Province of Holy Cross.

www.avemariapress.com

Paperback: ISBN-13 978-1-64680-377-4

E-book: ISBN-13 978-1-64680-378-1

Cover image © Massonstock / iStock / Getty Images Plus and Kubra Cavus / iStock / Getty Images Plus.

Cover and text design by Samantha Watson.

Printed and bound in the United States of America.

Library of Congress Cataloging-in-Publication Data is available.

For my spiritual sisters,
whose faith and friendship light the way.

Contents

Introduction

Aging Gracefully versus Aging with Grace

Since the publication of my first book, *My Badass Book of Saints*, I've entered into a new season of life. A milestone birthday ushered in a wave of physical, emotional, social, practical, and spiritual challenges. While my first book called upon extraordinary women and saints to show me how to live, I've found that what I need now is a host of saintly companions and courageous friends as I endeavor to age with grace.

One of my greatest challenges was the empty nest. The difficulty of launching our children out into the world stirred strong feelings in my marriage, although I understood it is all part of life. Even so, it was an adjustment for my husband and me to suddenly find ourselves back where we started. I couldn't remember how to cook for two, and found myself a little bored sometimes.

In time (and once John and I figured out how to buy groceries for two), however, other things fell neatly into place. We found ways to occupy our time, alone and together. It was a gift to our marriage to enjoy a regular date night (don't wait for the empty nest to do this!), and even though it seems a little cliché to share, we made the time to schedule vacations, including a lifelong dream of a pilgrimage to Rome.

Falling Into the Habit of Being

I was living my best life, enjoying travel and new hobbies, and not having to adhere to a schedule. I retired from teaching, moved to a downsized home along the Gulf Coast, and settled into our new community.

Over the course of just a few years, our children had moved away, pursuing their own dreams and careers, settling in different parts of the country, and starting their own families. At first, I floundered a bit, needing a sense of purpose. While I was delighted to formally retire from teaching, I found that I missed it. Not the stack of term papers that haunted my dreams, of course. But many mornings I woke up and wondered what I should do next.

My friends, some further along in this season of our lives, encouraged me to use this time to pray, and to be open to God's calling for me in this new time of my life. I joined a beautiful women's group, the Daughters of Mary, and I became a scheduled guardian and adorer at the Perpetual Adoration chapel in town. Taking care of myself spiritually led to a little self-care, too, but the greatest opportunity I had was to deepen my prayer life.

Discernment has always eluded me. It wasn't something that I heard when I was growing up, even in all the years I attended Catholic schools. I was unaware that as I spent many mornings in prayer pondering what my next thing would be, I was deep in discernment. I retired quite young, still in my fifties, and I while I appreciated the opportunity to pick up new hobbies, such as gardening, I had a sense that God wasn't finished with me yet, that perhaps there was still something meaningful I could do that utilized a lifetime of experience in education, writing, and public speaking.

As a writer, I had leveraged those things effectively in the vineyard, leading retreats, speaking at conferences, and of course, indulging in the joy of writing books; I even wrote a novel and wrote the script for the pilot of a children's animated series! Was that my Second Act? Was I going to pursue professional writing and public speaking? It was certainly an option. Unfortunately, my husband's health took a downturn, and while I retired from that public presence in social media while we figured out our next move, I felt unfulfilled, and even a little guilty that I had so many hours in a week that were spent navel-gazing at the end of a pier. To be clear, I thoroughly enjoyed this fallow period, but I always had the sense that God was working on me during that time. After all, you can't watch a sunrise over the Bay of the Holy Spirit and not feel the presence of our Creator God.

Embracing a Second Act

This sense of "fallowness" is something I've discovered in conversations with many friends, which often ended with (to quote C. S. Lewis in *The Four Loves*), "What? You too?" For many of us, this is the moment in which we find a true friend, an authentic connection with someone with whom we have an affinity. As we talk over this current period of transition, of feeling unseen and unheard, we find so many themes in common: The sense of drifting a little bit, busy with the demands on our time for our spouses, our adult children, and grandchildren. And perhaps the most common theme of all: how our days are often filled with activities, yet we often find ourselves alone.

Welcome to the "Second Act." It's a time of seemingly unending transition—for better, for worse, or just for *ever.* Whether we are thinking of actual retirement or just figuring out how to manage our current responsibilities given the challenges we are facing in other parts of our lives, we find ourselves continually pondering what we have to offer the world. We want to find ways to use our gifts and abilities to serve others, to cultivate a renewed sense of purpose.

In my case, it involved finding a new challenge—and when it finally came my way, I almost missed it! My inbox was always filled with job openings for educators, curriculum writers, mentors, trainers; all things I could do with one arm tied behind my back. So, when a brief email landed in my inbox asking for leads for an editor at CatholicMom.com, I deleted it without giving it a second thought. I'm embarrassed to admit this—after all, this was the first organization that gave me a platform to write about my faith. Unfortunately, I'm sometimes a little slow to recognize that God is speaking to me or giving me some direction, if only I would pay closer attention.

Five minutes later, I was sitting in Adoration asking God what he wanted me to do with all this time I had. I don't know why I was so emboldened in that hour, but I let him have it. I might have even chastised him, "Why can't you just send me an email with what you want from me!"

Yes, I really did say that.

I left Adoration having unburdened myself of my frustrations, and then sat in the hot car, scrolling through my email's trash looking for the email that was obviously meant for me. And with that, I entered my Second Act as an editor at CatholicMom.com. God is good like that. He uses everything that we experience and then says, "Here, fly!"

The women you are going to meet in this book come from a variety of backgrounds and life experiences—scientists and actresses and writers and religious. Some are canonized saints, others are heroes in a different sense. What they all have in common is they embraced the second half of life with courage, making the world a better place in the process.

Looking Heavenward to the Saints

If growing old gracefully was a goal powered by the desire to look and feel better physically and emotionally, then aging with grace—using my spiritual gifts to draw closer to the Lord—is even more important.

What our parents and grandparents experienced in the communal fold, with multiple generations living in close proximity, my generation is experiencing within an ever-shrinking nuclear family. The "heart space" that helped carry transitions is now borne by each of us individually.

The good news is that it doesn't have to be like that all the time. We can reclaim that "heart space" within us: our relationship with God, the Blessed Mother, and the Communion of Saints. As I began to face the changes and challenges of the second half of life, I turned to my "saint posse" to find just the right patron for what I was experiencing, confident I would find that "What, you too?" moment of connection with a holy model that would pray for me and show me a way to holiness.

As I turned again to the saints as companions on this journey, I discovered heavenly friends who provide consolation and advice, showing me by example how to live a holy life, how hardship and struggle can be beautiful opportunities for sanctification. My hope is that you find a friendly voice that echoes many of your experiences, and a source of encouragement as we all seek to age gracefully and with grace.

How to Use This Book

I hope that you find inspiration in this book. I hope your "What, you too?" moment jumps at you through these pages as you find a holy woman that inspires you and draws you closer to God, and closer to what he has in mind for you in *your* Second Act. At the very least, I hope you are entertained by some of the more obscure facts you may discover about these badass women and their saintly companions.

There's a brief section after each chapter that poses some questions for you to ponder. Ideally, you will take these to prayer and answer in your heart, or if you're like me, use them as a guided journal activity. You might also like to read this book within your circle of friends or as part of a book study and discuss your own "What, you too?" moments.

CHAPTER 1

A Stroke of Grace

Resilient Women Who Persevered

> "Every human being is an incalculable force, bearing within him something of the future. To the end of time, our daily words and actions will bear fruit, either good or bad; nothing that we have once given of ourselves will perish, but our words and works, handed on from one to another, will continue to do good or harm to remote generations. This is why life is a sacred thing, and we ought not to pass through it thoughtlessly, but to appreciate its value and use it so that, when we are gone, the sum total of good in the world may be greater."
> – Servant of God Elisabeth Leseur[1]

The year I turned forty-nine almost did me in. Literally. I had a mild stroke that both scared me and set me on a path to recover my health. Thankfully, there was no lasting visible damage from the stroke, but the secondary effects of renewed physical and spiritual attention gave me a new perspective, a wake-up call for the precious gift that is my life.

I was living with a lot of stress at the time. It seemed to me that the things I loved doing—teaching and personal endeavors in ministry and service—were always at odds. I felt devalued and unfulfilled because I had fallen into a rut and I didn't know how to get out of it. I grew up with the mindset that "winners never quit." Perseverance is an admirable virtue, but sometimes we persevere not as a virtuous struggle to attain the good, but as an exercise in pride in circumstances that are not good for us. That realization struck a chord and led to deep introspection and examination.

I wanted to fix what *I perceived* was broken, not considering that perhaps I was not equipped to do the fixing, or probably more likely, I was simply not a good fit. If the adage is true, with age comes wisdom, then I am a wise woman indeed to look back on that time of my life and realize I was suffering for no good reason, and it had affected my health to the point of elevated blood pressure. Finally, my stroke was like a warning shot across the bow of this ship I kept trying to right.

Kenny Rogers was right in his popular song "The Gambler." You do need to know when to "hold 'em" or "fold 'em." There was no running from this stroke—but I could learn to manage the stress so that I could walk forward with my head held high. Just like the women whose stories you will read in this chapter—and later in this book.

At the time, it seemed counterintuitive, even cowardly, to leave a situation that I believed was in need of correction. And yet, almost two decades later, I realize that all along God had been giving me signs that he had other things in store for me, and I needed to make room in my life for those.

Trying harder isn't always the answer.

Trying something new could be the answer. But that's scary. And hard. I was always the kid that had to learn the hard way, and that carried into adulthood, which led to suffering.

Now, in the abstract, I know that suffering is a part of life. I could teach a "master class" in suffering that would make my catechism teachers proud: I can quote the right scriptures, expound on passages from the *Catechism of the Catholic Church*, and even bring in a saint or two with wise words about the nature of suffering. And yet in order to truly understand suffering, we must start with the most basic, most enlightening fact: to know suffering, *we must ourselves suffer.*

The human condition is one of suffering; and yet, as Catholics we believe that what we do with our suffering is not just a test of our resilience, no matter what the world tells us with pithy memes and self-help books. To suffer is an invitation from God to join our pain and suffering to those of Christ upon the cross. To embrace suffering in this way elevates the experience above an earthly event that must be endured and sanctifies it in order to grow closer to Christ.

A Journey to Physical and Spiritual Health

For me, suffering a stroke proved to be a profound turning point in my physical and spiritual health. My journey to recovery may have begun in that moment of truth in the hospital, but it has been more than a dozen years of a daily recommitment to make better choices regarding my physical health—and even more my spiritual health.

I am in a season of my life where I have more years behind me than ahead of me. It's a sober realization that comes, not with anxiety and regret, but with the yearning to make the most of those years ahead. I held close to scripture, finding inspiration in Philippians 3:14: "I press on toward the goal, toward the prize of the heavenly call of God in Christ Jesus" (NRSV).

The catalyst to my Second Act, this frightening stroke that could have ended my life or set me on a very different course of recovery, became a blessing for me. In a very tangible, even miraculous way, God's mercy opened my eyes to the many changes I needed to make in my life to shift away from an existence that was filled with drudgery and self-imposed limitations to a life filled with hope and possibilities. I had an opportunity to begin again, as so many saints often exhorted. It didn't happen overnight; rather, it has been a journey of discovery and rediscovery as I work through this Second Act with my eyes on the prize.

In the subsequent years, I started preparing for a permanent move out of education. Did I suddenly quit my job and launch myself into the unknown? No. But I did have a change of attitude and a spiritual awakening, and *that* led to changes that were small and stretched out over a decade. Most teachers are vested in their pensions after thirty years but continue to work since they are ineligible to receive it until they turn sixty-two, while others take the early retirement and move on to other things.

I was firmly in the latter group, so I began to form a plan. I had the time to prepare for my Second Act. Of course, this isn't true for everyone—each woman enters her Second Act a bit differently. It is a time of transition marked by change, perseverance, and above all, faith.

I knew that my hobby of keeping a blog and publishing the occasional article could turn into my main focus. I had a window of time in which to develop my writing and build relationships in the publishing world. I didn't have to jump without a safety net, but it was a leap of faith nonetheless. I have never looked back.

Women of Hidden Genius

The women in this chapter seem to have little in common with each other, and yet they both had a kind of "hidden genius" that had long-reaching effects.

Hedy Lamarr left a burgeoning acting career in Europe when she was tricked into doing a morally compromising scene in a movie that subsequently tarred her reputation. Fortunately, she was able to reinvent herself in the United States, and her unexpected transformation from Hollywood actress to groundbreaking inventor is a brilliant example of latent genius transitioning into a remarkable Second Act.

Elisabeth Leseur suffered throughout her life, first as a devout Catholic married to an avowed atheist, and later with a terminal illness. Both Elisabeth and Hedy faced their challenges with a spirit of resilience in diverse contexts. They were intellectually brilliant and had an impact on the culture outside of their roles, breaking stereotypes while they lived and making an impact on the world after they died.

I identify with both these women, in different ways. Like Hedy Lamarr, I suffered in my career, never feeling I could reach my full potential, and yet, like her, I had a secret hobby that would prove to be the making of a Second Act. Elisabeth Leseur suffered both physical and spiritual crises, as I did.

Both these women had hidden lives where they expressed a fuller integration of who they were meant to be. Lamarr gained popularity and renown as an actress, while privately puttering around in a workshop creating world-changing inventions. Elisabeth Leseur, like so many saints before her, lived a quiet life of heroic virtue, turning to the Lord in a secret diary where she was able to be fully who she was and *whose* she was. No one would know of this hidden part of her life until her death. Both women have received recognition posthumously, proving that their Second Acts, begun late in life, continue to have an impact today.

Hedy Lamarr: Stunning Star, Serious Scientist

Hedy Lamarr was born Hedwig Maria Kiesler on November 9, 1914, in Vienna, Austria. Her father was a successful banker and her mother was a musician. They fostered intellectual curiosity in their daughter, and not only did she take ballet lessons and piano, but she was encouraged to tinker with technical gadgets, too.

Lamarr attended a drama school and started to get roles in European films. One of those films cast her in the role of ingenue, but the director shifted a scene to capitalize on an explicit sexual theme. Unfortunately for Lamarr, the film received international notoriety because of its controversial content, and she had a difficult time facing the consequences, particularly in her marriage. She disappeared to Paris and then London, both to escape the unwanted attention from the film and to leave her unhappy marriage to a munitions dealer.

In London, she met Louis B. Mayer, cofounder of MGM Studios, who invited her to Hollywood. How could she say no? She immediately starred in a series of successful movies capitalizing on her exotic beauty and incredible acting talent. My mother was a fan of classic movies, and I remember watching with her one of Lamarr's films, *Samson and Delilah*. Later, I took a film class in college and my professor was enamored with Lamarr; that is where I first learned there was more to her than meets the eye.

Despite her Hollywood success, Lamarr felt unfulfilled with the glamor and cookie-cutter roles she played. Science and invention were where her real passion led her, and she entertained herself with little inventions that she pursued on the side. Yet no one knew about this side of her, because it contrasted with her public image of Hollywood starlet.

Lamarr's popularity as an actress allowed her to move in social circles not only within Hollywood but also beyond it among the wealthy and high society. She dated many men and was married and divorced six times (including her first husband in Austria). One of her more interesting relationships was with Howard Hughes, who gave her the intellectual stimulation she craved and provided her with a resource table with tools that she could keep on set so she could fiddle with gadgets and gizmos while filming.[2] Because of Hughes's fascination with planes, Lamarr studied both fish and birds to find a new wing design for Hughes. Talk about breaking stereotypes about "shallow" actresses!

A few years later, as World War II loomed, a chance encounter with musician and composer George Antheil created an unlikely partnership that enabled them both to support the war cause. Antheil's understanding of sound waves, together with Lamarr's familiarity with munitions (which she picked up while married to her first husband), led to a collaboration for a device the navy could use to find submarines. It was an instrument that allowed both receiver and transmitter to hop frequencies.[3] In 1997, Lamarr and Antheil were given the Pioneer Award for their work on that frequency hopping transmitter/receiver. In 2014 she was posthumously inducted into the National Inventors Hall of Fame for developing the technology that led to the creation of GPS technology and Wi-Fi! Hedy Lamarr might have wanted to be an actress, but it was her Second Act, seeking fulfillment in what she found inspiring and challenging, that left a mark on this earth.

As a result of these awards, Hedy Lamarr became the subject of renewed interest. Her story served as inspiration for young women to enter the fields of science and technology. She became a powerful reminder that intellectual pursuits should not be confined by societal expectations, even though Lamarr herself was held back by those very restrictions.

Despite those challenges, Lamarr demonstrated not only resilience but an ability to reinvent herself. I was surprised to learn that the Catwoman character from DC Comics' Batman series was inspired by Hedy Lamarr.[4] Another Hollywood star, Anne Hathaway, based her depiction of Catwoman in *The Dark Knight Rises* on Hedy Lamarr.[5]

Hedy's Hollywood legacy and her contribution to science and technology have both been captured in a documentary film, *Bombshell: The Hedy Lamarr Story*, in which she is celebrated for her intellect, resilience, and ability to break from society's expectations. She is credited with saying, "Films have a certain place in a certain time period. Technology is forever."[6] Her popularity in Hollywood waned after the 1950s, but she entered her Second Act fiercely, dedicating herself to inventions and developing technology.

Some women, like Hedy Lamarr, enjoy the limelight and live very public lives with a private life hidden from view. Other women, such as Servant of God Elisabeth Leseur, live quiet lives of contemplation and reserve. What is perhaps most remarkable about both women, who lived in times when society's expectations limited their options, is that they continued to change the world even after their deaths.

Servant of God Elisabeth Leseur: Beacon of Love and Faith

Elisabeth Arigghi was born on October 16, 1866, in Paris, France. Raised in a well-to-do, devoutly Catholic household, Elisabeth spoke several languages fluently and had a great deal of curiosity. Her upbringing instilled in her a strong foundation in the faith, which would play out later in her life.

As a young woman, she met her husband, Felix, who was visiting extended family next door. Felix Leseur was a physician and intellectual, and they made a good match. They were married in 1889, a loving union based upon mutual respect. However, Felix was a staunch atheist—he had lost his faith at university, where he had absorbed the anticlericalism and anti-Catholicism that ran rampant during that time (as it often does today). A devout Catholic, Elisabeth didn't discover how deep his convictions were rooted until right before the wedding.

This impasse would prove a trial for Elisabeth in her marriage. When she first discovered his lack of faith, Felix assured Elisabeth that he would not get in the way of her own faith. Unfortunately, as time went on, he began to pick at her beliefs, mocking her practice of the faith and becoming hostile to her Catholicism. Their friends, too, were mostly other atheists from the university.

Slowly, Felix removed any opportunity for Elisabeth to share her faith or even practice devotions in her home. He effectively ruined her ability to pray by destroying her peace. When Felix thought he was close to winning her over, he gave her two popular books that took a stand against Christianity: *The Origins of Christianity* and *The Life of Jesus*. Reading these books should have been the final blow to what was left of Elisabeth's faith, but they had the opposite effect. Rather than accept the arguments presented in the books as fact, Elisabeth began to study to find the truth for herself.

She began with the New Testament, and she discovered Jesus Christ himself in a way she had not known him before. Her confidence in Christ could not be shaken, though she had to continue to live her faith in the face of her husband's hostility.

Inevitably, Felix discovered that his tactic had failed, and Elisabeth had found a new and deeper spirituality. He doubled down on his criticism of the faith, and his attacks became even more critical. Elisabeth withdrew, not wanting to continue arguing. She took her faith to an interior place and began journaling, where she could not only process the changes in her life but also explore, freely, her faith. Meanwhile, the couple's outward life continued, with their social calls and interaction with extended family.

Elisabeth's Second Act: A Life of Hidden Intercession

Elisabeth's health was a source of ongoing challenge for the couple. Early in their marriage, they discovered that Elisabeth was unable to bear children because of an infection. And although they were spared the conflicts that arise between parents when only one wants to raise a child in the faith, it was a terrible heartache for them. Unable to bear a child, Elisabeth made it her plan to love the children in her family and circle.

Elisabeth and Felix were determined that their marriage would be a mutual experience of love, sacrifice, loss, and joy, even when Elisabeth's poor health sometimes affected her ability to get out of the house. She stated, "It is quite clear to me that the divine will for me is not in action. Until further notice, I must confine myself almost exclusively to prayer and endeavor to possess more the spirit of sacrifice."[7] Felix, too, sacrificed in the marriage, as he gave up his dreams of travel. Despite his disregard for the Church, he made it possible for his wife to receive the sacraments in her illness.

Elisabeth's journals and diaries capture the depth of her faith, and the depth of her love for her husband. She wrote extensively on the power of prayer. She prayed fervently for her husband, specifically for him to have a spiritual conversion, and she prayed for others who had also left the faith. She understood the power of offering up her own suffering for the conversion of others, and meditated often on aligning her suffering to Christ's as an opportunity for spiritual growth. Finally, she recognized that love was the central message of the Gospels, and through love expressed in all the ways one loves in a marriage, would be the most powerful testimony of faith.

Elisabeth died at the age of forty-seven. Felix found her writings and letters, and was convicted by *her* faith. He had a profound conversion, first touched by her love for him and then surprised by a letter addressed to him that detailed his conversion. He did, indeed, have a reversion to the faith, and he went on to become a priest. He spent the rest of his life preparing her papers in the hopes that she would one day be canonized a saint. He already knew the miracle of his own conversion.

Elisabeth's spirituality and writings reflected a deep love of the Eucharist as well as prayer life and meditation. Her diary is a source of inspiration today. It is a beautiful snapshot of marriage, and an incredible window into the power of prayer.

Both Elisabeth Leseur and Hedy Lamarr were remarkable women who exemplified resilience and innovation. Hedy Lamarr enjoyed a Hollywood career that overshadowed her gift with technology, a gift that she largely kept private until an opportunity presented itself to reveal it. Elisabeth Leseur left a spiritual gold mine in her diaries and writings that inspire generations with her reflections on prayer, love, and spirituality.

Both women left a legacy, a Second Act that plays out in others through their influence, and an inspiration for women who find themselves living in circumstances that limit them in some way. I look to them as inspiration in my own life, a reminder that we all have within us not only resilience but the capacity for creative change in our lives to keep growing, and with the grace of faith, to bring light into the world within our own circles of influence.

QUESTIONS TO PONDER

1. Have you ever felt that you could not express a part of yourself? What did you do?

2. What role does resilience play in your life?

3. How do you process your spiritual life? Do you turn to Adoration? Prayer? Spiritual journaling?

CHAPTER 2

Pioneering Scientists
Who Kept Their Minds Strong

"Dare to declare who you are. It is not far from the shores
of silence to the boundaries of speech. The path is not
long, but the way is deep. You must not only walk there,
you must be prepared to leap."

–St. Hildegard of Bingen[1]

The Trappist monastery close to my home turned into an oasis of
peace for me. It was one of my favorite places to go, especially if
I had a day off in the middle of the week. Acres and acres of land
called to me for exploration, and I would take long walks along its
perimeter. I had full access to the abbey church, but the cloistered
part was always a mystery to me. I tried to catch a glimpse of what
was on the other side of the walls where shrubbery was used as
a natural barrier, or where a brick wall used a pattern that wasn't
completely closed. At most, I saw a monk walking on a path to an
unknown destination. The mystery was alluring.

On more than one occasion, I wondered what it might be like to live in a world exclusively of prayer and work, *ora et labora*, as I saw in little signs in the garden. It was an intrusive thought, probably the result of a busy season in my life when I would yearn for the quiet respite of the monastery. Then, I would return to whatever madness waited for me in the bustle of a home filled with teenagers or the overwhelming demands of finals week or fall registration at the college.

Before I left the peace and quiet of my temporary vacation, I would slip into the bookstore for a little window shopping, wishing I had the budget to buy some of the exquisite artwork for sale. The usual statues and icons you would expect to find in a monastery store were there, but the monks specialized in stained-glass windows and sand casts, so there was always something special that I wanted. Of course, there were books, and those usually broke my budget. Nevertheless, I never left without buying something to support them, even if it was only a holy card. The checkout area was always filled with little tchotchkes, coins and bracelets with Bible verses, the random chaplet or Sacred Heart car magnet.

On one occasion, I noticed a box filled with cookies. That looked like a good idea; I would have a snack on the way home. I grabbed one absentmindedly—the monks were master fudge makers; perhaps now they were now making cookies.

I was gravely mistaken.

I realized my mistake the moment I got to the car and took a closer look at the packaging: something billed as Hildegard of Bingen's "Nerve Cookie." That should have been warning enough, but then I read the packaging: no eggs, no butter, no sugar . . . no taste. I thought, "What the heck, my nerves are shot anyway, I might as well eat it."

I thought I was going to get some variety of oatmeal cookie. Nope. It was like eating a slice of tree bark. It was bad. Dry, and not at all a texture I would associate with a cookie or even a cracker. I guess the peasants didn't know any better a thousand years ago. I drove home with the aftertaste of mealy sawdust in my mouth, but I kept the insert in the package that had the recipe on one side and a little bit of Hildegard's history on the other side. Get this, the cookies were also called Hildegard of Bingen's "Cookies of Joy." (Joy Suckers, more like.) Had I grabbed a batch that had been in storage too long?

My curiosity was piqued, so I took a closer look at the wrapper and found this explanation from St. Hildegard herself:

> Take some nutmeg and an equal weight of cinnamon and a bit of cloves, and pulverize them. Then make small cakes with this and fine whole wheat flour and water. Eat them often. It will calm all bitterness of the heart and mind, open your heart and impaired senses, and make your mind cheerful. It purifies your senses and diminishes all harmful humors in you. It gives good liquid to your blood, and makes you strong. (*Physica*, ca. 1151–1158)

"Okay," I thought, "I could use some good liquid in my blood. Perhaps I do need this." But what would happen if I added a little brown sugar? She probably just didn't have brown sugar in 1158. By the way, the internet is filled with variations of this recipe. You can see for yourself what I'm talking about. She also made wine. Stay away.

And thus began my fascination with Hildegard of Bingen, a saint who wasn't formally canonized until 2012, when Pope Benedict XVI declared that she was traditionally a saint, anyway, so let's formalize it. That same year he also made her a Doctor of the Church, upping the number of female Doctors of the Church to four. I needed to know more about this woman.

Getting to the Root of It All

At this point in my life, I was experiencing a number of health crises, most of which were self-induced due to stress at work and poor eating habits. I had high blood pressure, mood swings, pre-diabetes, obesity, and to cap it all off, I was also in the throes of perimenopause. I. Was. A. Mess. Maybe a little nerve cookie was just what the doctor ordered.

Thanks to the success of my first book, *My Badass Book of Saints*, I had developed a reputation for distilling life lessons from unusual and little-known Catholic saints and strong women (Catholic or not) who did extraordinary things. I looked to these women as mentors. I'm a woman who hopes one day to be a saint—if not the canonized type, at least the kind that makes it to heaven.

Now, as I enter my *Second* Act, I find myself drawn to women and saints who did extraordinary things late in life. They remind me that retirement isn't an end, it's an opportunity for transition—as in Hildegard of Bingen's life, which was really a parade of exploring all her interests! Good ole Hildy did it all, satisfying her curiosity and moving on to the third, fifth, tenth act that inspired her.

Then one day I *rediscovered* Madame Marie Curie, the Nobel-winning physicist (who was merely a paragraph in my high school physics book), when she resurfaced in a fascinating article about her lab books, which are still radioactive and locked away (apparently you can touch them if you sign a release).[2]

These women made pioneering contributions to science, spanning different historical periods and scientific disciplines. Marie Curie's groundbreaking work in modern physics aligns with St. Hildegard's medieval contributions to various fields, including the natural sciences. They are examples of endurance. Rather than peaking early, both women *were* ready to embrace the next great thing, moving through their lives in a vibrant race to the finish. Whatever it is that inspires me next, I hope to pursue it with their level of curiosity and perseverance.

Madame Marie Curie: Scientist, Researcher, Extraordinary Woman

Maria Sklodowska was born on November 7 in 1878 in Warsaw, Poland. Her mother and older sister died when she was very young, leaving her in her father's care. She attended local schools, but it was her father who introduced her to the study of science. She was raised in a devout Catholic family where faith and other virtues such as compassion and service were instilled.

For the young Marie, science complemented her faith. She had a keen curiosity about the world and became a diligent student—so diligent, in fact, that she often missed meals and slept very little. This resonates with me, as I was a very curious child. When I learned to read at an unusually young age, it opened up the world of imagination along with a thirst to read about history and world cultures. Unlike Curie, though, I was undisciplined. I never missed a meal (I brought the book to the table only to be reprimanded) but I did skimp on chores, drawing my mother's ire.

Despite her excellent work ethic and academic preparation, as a woman Marie was denied admission to the universities near her. I can't imagine the let-down for someone so dedicated to learning.

It led to a mental breakdown, no doubt fueled by disappointment, and she became a governess.[3]

Reading her story, I can't help but wonder what else has been lost to us because women were not encouraged to fulfill goals and use gifts that did not fit neatly within society's expectations. Thankfully, Curie persevered, and in 1891 she enrolled at the Sorbonne in Paris to study chemistry and physics. Within several years she received her credentials and became a professor. In 1894 she met and married Pierre Curie, who was also a professor. They became a formidable team, collaborating on scientific research.

Together with another scientist, Henri Becquerel, the Curies discovered and explored the properties of radiation, which laid the foundation for later study in the field of nuclear physics. By 1898, they had isolated two new elements: polonium and radium. With Becquerel, they received the Nobel Prize in Physics in 1903, a special distinction for her as the first woman to ever win a Nobel Prize. It came with international notoriety, too, as the world reacted to a woman excelling in this field.

This pioneering research also laid the groundwork for further research in the field of oncology, as radiation therapy became an essential therapy in the fight against cancer. Ironically, it would be cancer that took Marie's life.

Marie's Second Act

Tragically, Pierre Curie was killed in a traffic accident in 1906. Undeterred, Marie took over his position as professor of physics at the Sorbonne (the first woman ever to achieve this position) and continued their research. She then became director of the Curie Laboratory at the Radium Institute of the University of Paris. In 1911, she received a second Nobel Prize, this time in chemistry.

Although she earned many distinctions in her lifetime, she faced just as many hardships. She overcame the prohibition against attending university in Poland by moving to France, but that didn't mean it would be an easy path for her there. She continued to experience discrimination for working in a male-dominated field. Nevertheless, she remained steadfast in her work and relentlessly pursued excellence. Despite a scandal due to a short-lived love affair with a married colleague that threatened her career and almost cost her the second Nobel Prize, Curie returned to the values she learned as a young girl and continued to serve the world through her gifts.

Marie Curie died of leukemia on July 4, 1934. It is believed she contracted leukemia as a result of her lifetime exposure to radiation. In 1995, her remains were moved to the French National Mausoleum, the first time a woman was interred there for her own merit. Her legacy as a scientist and as a woman serves as a model for the transformative power of perseverance in pushing the boundaries of knowledge. She pushed herself first and never stopped.

St. Hildegard of Bingen: A Pre-Renaissance Woman

If Marie Curie is a model of lifelong study and inquiry in pursuit of knowledge, then St. Hildegard of Bingen was the original mold. A formidable woman known as much for her musical art as for her healing and medical knowledge (even if her cookies were a little on the dry side), Hildegard was born in Bockelheim, North Franconia, in what is today Germany, in 1098. Raised in a twelfth-century noble family, Hildegard was given to the Catholic Church *as a tithe*.

Child oblation, as it is often called, was the practice of turning over a child to a monastery as a gift to God, and had roots in the biblical story of Hannah, who gave her son Samuel up for service to God. Eight-year-old Hildegard was offered to the local Benedictine monastery in the same way. This seemed to work in Hildegard's favor, freeing her from the obligations a woman might have had at the time. It came with a few perks as well: at a time when most women couldn't write (the primary reason we don't hear more about women from the twelfth century and earlier), Hildegard was a prolific writer.

Hildegard was placed in the guardianship of Jutta of Sponheim for her spiritual formation and education. Even as a child, Hildegard demonstrated a keen intelligence, as well as a deep devotion coupled with mystical visions. As she grew older, she would refer to these visions as *revelations*, and they became a foundational point of her spirituality and writings.

Themes such as the nature of God and the nature of creation gave her an appreciation for the natural world as sacred. Although I laughed at the idea of nerve cookies, Hildegard was millennia ahead of the current trend of holistic healing that integrates the medicinal plants God gave us in the world with the spiritual component of healing through presence in the natural world and prayer.

A logical and complementary study of music rounded out Hildegard's interests. She was an accomplished musician and prolific composer of hymns and antiphons. Her body of work includes liturgical music that is not only still performed today, but studied for its innovative structures and unique blending of Gregorian chant with her own compositions. Hildegard viewed music as the avenue to express the beauty of the Divine.

Hildegard's Second Act

St. Hildegard was driven by curiosity about the world around her. Although she also exhibited a keen leadership in a period when women rarely had such opportunities, it was her wonder at the natural world that inspired me.

Hildegard's work ethic is manifest in her prolific writings in the fields of music, theology, medicine, healing, and spirituality, which make up a remarkable body of work that justifies her being named a Doctor of the Church. Yet this is not where her story ends. Even as she wrote about and pursued a diversity of interests and creative projects, Hildegard faced a backlash from ecclesiastical authorities who were upset that a woman was daring to operate outside the social norms.

In 1150, Hildegard founded her own religious community in Rupertsberg. She wanted to establish a convent where women could not only pursue a life of prayer but also commit to serving and learning. The abbot at the monastery of Disibodenberg, where Hildegard had lived all these years, denied her request. Undaunted, she went over his head and appealed to the archbishop, who granted her request. The community was a success under Hildegard's leadership, and its numbers grew, making a second community a possibility.

Many years later, a man who had been excommunicated died and Hildegard allowed him to be buried in their convent cemetery. Scandalized, the local clergy demanded his body be exhumed. Hildegard refused, claiming that the man had reconciled himself with the Church shortly before his death. The local priest insisted upon the removal of the man's remains, and still Hildegard refused on grounds of charity.

The next morning, when the priest returned with a crew to remove the man's remains, he discovered that all the grave markers had been removed, so there was no way to determine where the man had been buried. (I shouldn't laugh, but if I could give the sisters a high five, I would.) St. Hildegard showed great tenacity and creativity in deterring what she felt was an egregious lack of charity.

St. Hildegard of Bingen was a force to be reckoned with. We know of other great female saints who had the same moxie, the same confidence in their authority and the strength of their convictions. St. Teresa of Avila founded convents and monasteries; St. Catherine of Siena corresponded with kings and popes. But St. Hildegard predated them both by three hundred years! Her circle of influence included popes, bishops, emperors, and other important men; she offered them all her counsel and vision, and they respected her for her wisdom and creativity as well as her unwavering faith.

I tremble at the thought that, had her parents not given her to the Church, we might never have known the brilliance of St. Hildegard of Bingen. She simply followed the path God had prepared for her. And when we celebrate women such as Marie Curie, who refused to have her goals limited because of gender, we are emboldened to embrace *our own* goals as we enter this Second Act of life.

QUESTIONS TO PONDER

1. Do you feel inspired to continue in your chosen vocation or avocation as you enter your Second Act, or do you see this as an opportunity to discover new things?

2. Where do you draw your strength from? Prayer? Devotions? Other practices?

3. Can you name one new thing that you would like to explore as part of your Second Act?

CHAPTER 3

Visionary Leaders

Who Were Unafraid to Kick Butt and Take Names

"I have learned to know God, and am glad for it. If you know him, you too will rejoice."

–St. Olga of Kyiv[1]

I'm a royal watcher. I feel a little silly making this confession, but there it is: I'm fascinated with the British monarchy. I watched *The Crown* in its entirety. I think Helen Mirren made a great Queen Elizabeth II in *The Queen*. Like so many young women in 1981, I got up at dawn to watch Lady Diana walk down the aisle and marry her prince, and I wept in 1997 when I heard she had died.

I'm a little less interested in the younger royals, but whenever something pops up in my feed, I will indulge myself and go down the rabbit hole for a little while. I just love the pomp and circumstance, the beautiful ball gowns, and the military uniforms.

Perhaps it speaks to the fairy tales I enjoyed as a little girl, but I should probably also point out that my mom and her girlfriends would pass along the latest copies of *Hola!* magazine, which was a never-ending parade of European royalty. There's something about tradition and pageantry that I find enthralling.

The fictionalized accounts of Queen Elizabeth's life generally send me to the history books in search of the grain of truth in the stories. The bottom line is that I had great admiration for the queen. I know there's a controversial aspect to the monarchy. As an immigrant, I have a family history of oppression, from colonialization to civil war, so I am sympathetic to those who believe that a monarchy, particularly the British monarchy, is a source of oppression.

Still, I'm fascinated by stories of women rulers of their own kingdoms (not simply figureheads or consorts). History is filled with stories of women who were rulers effecting great things for their people, many attaining greatness despite a prevailing culture that oppressed women or limited their reach.

My own education focused on western history and culture, so naturally, Queen Elizabeth II of the United Kingdom stands out for me, a woman who was not born to be queen, but rose to the occasion with elegance and class, and in her own lifetime instituted changes in the rules of succession to allow for women to ascend to the throne as rightful heirs despite younger male siblings. She served in the military, traveled extensively, and, although the decolonization and independence of many nations held under British rule had begun before she was born, saw a greater movement toward independence in her lifetime.

Queens and rulers from other time periods and parts of the world also piqued my interest. These strong women ruled despite male-dominated cultures, and yet they advocated for breaking gender-related barriers while being comprehensive rulers for their countries.

- *Hatshepsut* (ruling 1479–1458 BC) ruled Egypt as one of the most successful pharaohs, expanding trade and building monumental architecture.
- *Wu Zetian*, the first and only female emperor of China (ruling AD 690–705), changed policies to improve the status of women, appointed women to the courts, and encouraged education of girls and women.
- *Lady Six Sky* (Lady Wac Chanil Ahau) was a warrior queen who ruled the Mayan territories (seventh century AD) as a powerful and successful ruler.
- *Nur Jahan* ruled India beside her husband (AD 1611–1627), issuing currency, owning ships for trade, and advocating for women to participate in society outside the home.
- *Queen Nzinga* ruled Angola (AD 1624–1663), resisting Portuguese colonization and playing a key role in the preservation of her people and culture.

And finally, *Queen Liliʻuokalani* of Hawaii ruled AD 1891–1893 as the last sovereign of the Kamehameha dynasty, overthrown during the US annexation of Hawaii. These were mature women who used their power not only to rule their country, but protect and build up their culture.

In this chapter I explore the reign of Queen Liliʻuokalani of Hawaii and what her people meant to her, as well as a wild story of St. Olga of Kyiv, whose ferocious pagan rule saw an astounding Second Act filled with a conversion to Christianity and the spiritual transformation that led to the conversion of Kievan Rus. Hold onto your hats for that story.

Queen Lili'uokalani of Hawaii: Protector of Her People

I first learned about Queen Lili'uokalani from a native Hawaiian Facebook friend who shared that she was embarking on a pilgrimage of sorts, following in the footsteps of Hawaii's Queen Kapi'olani and her daughter Princess Lili'uokalani, who had traveled to meet Queen Victoria of England. The pilgrimage took her across the Pacific to California, across the United States to the East Coast, and across the Atlantic to England. I was enthralled by the pilgrimage, but more amazed by the story of two queens meeting each other.

Lydia Lili'u Loloku Walania Wewehi Kamaka'eha was born on September 2, 1838, in Honolulu, Oahu. She was born into the royal family of Kamehameha, and during her childhood was steeped in traditional Hawaiian culture as well as Western culture.

In Lili'uokalani's lifetime, the Hawaiian Kingdom was recognized internationally; it had treaties around the world, dozens of embassies, state neutrality, and over a hundred years before the United States it had universal suffrage as well as universal healthcare. She attended the Royal School, which was established by American missionaries, and she received a well-rounded education that included, in addition to the traditional reading, writing, and mathematical curriculum, musical and religious training.

Lili'uokalani was an accomplished musician and composer, and I was surprised to learn that she was the composer of "Aloha Oe," the song that is so connected with Hawaii and known throughout the world. She played the piano, guitar, and ukelele beautifully, and used Western and Hawaiian musical themes and traditions to create a blended style that has left an enduring legacy. She was training to one day become queen.

Unfortunately, when King Kamehameha died, he left no clear successor, and the legislature selected the next king. Lili'uokalani's brother David became king. Because he traveled abroad, Lili'uokalani often served as regent, and after his death in 1891, when she was well into her fifties, she became queen.

Lili'uokalani's reign was not easy, as there were efforts to eliminate the monarchy. In fact, one of her goals when she became queen was to upend the existing Hawaiian constitution that limited the monarchy and thereby gave bargaining and trade power to American and European business investors. The Bayonet Constitution, created in 1887, had limited her brother's influence as king, and in 1898 Hawaii was annexed to the United States. In 1893, Lili'uokalani proposed a new constitution that would restore the monarchy to its original state and restore voting rights to disenfranchised native Hawaiian and Asian citizens, but it was met with strong opposition from American businessmen under the guise of the Committee of Safety, which executed a coup d'etat with the support of the United States minister to Hawaii and US Marines from the USS Boston.

Lili'uokalani believed that President Grover Cleveland would support her reinstatement as queen as soon as he found out how this group of opportunists had overthrown her. So convinced was she of this support from the president that she surrendered peacefully, to prevent bloodshed.

President Cleveland did indeed support her and tried to have her restored to power, but the political situation shifted in Washington, DC, and the new president, William McKinley, sided with the American interests in favor of annexation of Hawaii. Queen Lili'uokalani was put under house arrest; when her confinement was relaxed, she traveled to the United States to plead her case. She wanted justice for Hawaii.

In 1895, royalists launched a counterrevolution that failed and resulted in Lili'uokalani's imprisonment in her own palace, and she was charged with insurrection. It was during this imprisonment that she composed many beautiful songs and wrote her memoir, *Hawaii's Story by Hawaii's Queen*, published in 1898, the same year the annexation was finalized and Hawaii became part of the United States.

A Brief but Important Second Act

Lili'uokalani's reign was brief, but not without great influence. The people of Hawaii appreciated the risks she took, even while attempting to spare her people bloodshed. While imprisoned, she did everything she could to reverse the injustices perpetrated against the Hawaiian Kingdom, sending the following letter to President McKinley of the United States, in a final appeal for justice in 1897:

> I, Lili'uokalani of Hawaii . . . do hereby protest against the ratification of a certain treaty, which . . . has been signed at Washington . . . purporting to cede those Islands to the territory and dominion of the United States. I declare such a treaty to be an act of wrong toward the native and part-native people of Hawaii, an invasion of the rights of the ruling chiefs, in violation of international rights both toward my people and toward friendly nations with whom they have made treaties, the perpetuation of the fraud whereby the constitutional government was overthrown, and, finally, an act of gross injustice to me.[2]

She died on November 11, 1917, at the age of seventy-nine. She is revered still today for her efforts at maintaining the Hawaiian

Kingdom, her dedication to the people, and her cultural contributions in history and music. She remains a symbol of resistance against imperialist forces and the annexation of Hawaii by what turned out to be trickery for the purpose of personal advancement.

Even though Lili'uokalani lost everything important to her—the monarchy, the sovereignty of her country, even her freedom—she never lost her love for her people and culture, and that has remained as her legacy. When we look for role models or exceptional people to emulate, we tend to think in terms of winning. Lili'uokalani was not successful in protecting her kingdom, and yet she should be remembered for fighting the good fight and seeking justice for her people.

St. Olga of Kyiv: Dragonslayer

Queen Olga of Kyiv was a scary woman. Scary like *Game of Thrones* scary. St. Olga was an important figure in the history of Kievan Rus, the eastern Slavic state that we know as Ukraine today. Known for extreme brutality, her dramatic conversion to Christianity had an impact on her kingdom. Mild-mannered Queen Lili'uokalani loved her people (and was loved in return) and dealt peacefully with political opposition. Queen Olga? She exemplifies one of the most dramatic one-eightys in history. I'd say she exemplifies the change that is possible when a person surrenders their whole being to the will of God.

Most of Olga's life was undocumented because of the time in which she lived. She was born around AD 890, and was married to the grand prince of Kyiv, Igor. While traveling through the countryside on a tax-collecting mission in 945, Prince Igor was murdered by a neighboring tribe, the Drevlians. As a result, Olga became regent until their young son was old enough to rule. And she pledged revenge for her husband's brutal murder. He had been torn apart with bent trees, and Olga planned to exact retribution for this heinous act.

The Drevlians were just not prepared for the brutality that Olga was about to rain upon them. First, the Drevlians sent their emissaries with an ambassador, thinking they had the upper hand on a grieving widow. They proposed she marry their prince to unify the kingdoms. Instead, Olga had them buried alive.

A second contingent went to Kyiv, and Olga welcomed them in a huge show of hospitality. Because they did not know the fate of the first group, they accepted her invitation to bathe and rest in a bathhouse. As soon as they were inside, she barred the doors and had them burned alive.

Then, Olga took her own contingent of soldiers to the Drevlian capital of Iskorosten, where she held an enormous feast to celebrate her late husband and invited the Drevlians. She proceeded with her plan to get them all drunk, and then had her soldiers slaughter every last one of them. Around five thousand Drevlian men were killed.

At this point, I think the Drevlians should have moved.

The final act was probably the most cunning: Olga's men attacked Iskorosten, and were of course met with a counterattack. The siege was not meant to be successful, but rather to establish a standoff between the warring parties. At that point, Olga suggested a peace offering. She asked for three pigeons and three sparrows from each house as tribute. She had the birds fitted with incendiary materials and released them so that they returned to their homes and nests. As a result, the thousands of returning birds set the entire city of Iskorosten on fire, immolating the city and its inhabitants.

Of course, this scenario is horrific. Our Christian sensibilities balk at the thought of Olga escalating violence against her enemies, the Drevlians. But consider the context of those times. Were her actions motivated by evil and brutality for its own sake? Or was she a cunning leader who understood how to establish herself as a force to be reckoned with, thereby protecting her kingdom and her son?

Queen Olga's Second Act

A dozen years after the destruction of the Drevlians, in 957, Olga's life made a complete turnaround. She converted to Christianity, traveled to Constantinople, the heart of the Byzantine Empire, and was baptized as a Christian. Her godfather was Emperor Constantine VII.

What happened during those twelve years? Clearly, Olga experienced a conversion, but her actions also had clever political implications. Aligning herself with Constantinople and the Byzantine Empire gave Kyiv political legitimacy, military and trade alliances, and other strategic advantages. Was it a political choice or a spiritual choice? I think this Second Act was a true conversion—and so does the Church, canonizing her in 1547 in the Eastern Rite.

St. Olga's initial conversion and baptism might have looked like political theater, but her actions speak differently. She seemed genuinely drawn to the Christian faith, as she participated in spreading Christianity within her realm. Although Olga's son remained a pagan, her actions laid the groundwork for the Christianization of the entire region.

St. Olga built churches. She invited priests to her court. She celebrated her Christianity publicly, in the court and in the towns, and introduced Christian customs, practices, and teachings throughout the region. Her son may have remained pagan, but her grandson, Vladimir the Great, adopted Christianity as the official state religion in 988, defining the spiritual identity of Kievan Rus.

It's true that Olga's early story was filled with brutality, but her legacy heralded a Christian era in Eastern Europe. Her motives are often questioned, her sincerity suspect, but how is she different from any other sinner who repents, turns away from sin, and believes in the Gospel? St. Olga had the most spectacular Second Act, and her legacy continues to be a force in the world.

QUESTIONS TO PONDER

1. Does Christianity demand of us success or conviction?
2. What does the Catholic faith teach about repentance?
3. What do you find most inspiring about these women?

CHAPTER 4

Dedicated Mothers

Who Embodied "Love in the Trenches"

"I am hungry for the work. I am not afraid of any disease."

–St. Marianne Cope[1]

My earliest memories of Christmas include going shopping with my mother to buy a gift for a local toy drive. We may have gone to Toys for Tots; it was already around in the 1960s. The fact that I remember tells me it is a core memory, that it left a lasting mark on me. Years later, when I got to high school, I volunteered for service organizations, and as an adult, I joined the Society of St. Vincent de Paul, using my bilingual skills to help the underserved Spanish-speaking clients.

When I volunteered at my parish, I loved speaking with the folks who came to our office. Most were looking for groceries to help tide them over until they got a paycheck; others, with more serious needs, asked for help with their water or power bills to have service restored. Most came in humbled by their need. A very few might have acted angry or entitled, but those were rare cases. Regardless, it was our job and our joy to be kind and helpful, and to treat them with the dignity they deserved.

Some say that volunteering with service organizations sanitizes the experience of helping the poor, who come to us in our offices, in our comfort zones, where applications and prepackaged, uniform resources are distributed. Although it puts the onus of discomfort on those who already bear a burden of need, and probably also bear the stigma of poverty, I believe it is an important process. It is no small thing that volunteering in such centers can be a gateway experience to greater sympathy all around. I wish there was a better way.

The alternative is to go where there is a need. Many people find the strength of character to do so. I am not one of those people. I am not afraid, or put off, or biased. On the contrary, I become useless and ineffective because I am overcome with feelings, and I become a liability. I would have made a terrible missionary, and yet I know that the only way to get comfortable outside my comfort zone is to allow myself to get uncomfortable.

When my children were in high school, I accompanied one of them on a youth group day-mission to work in a soup kitchen in downtown Atlanta. They needed drivers, and a few adults pooled our minivans and off we went. I had no expectations; I really went along to drive. Imagine my surprise when the director of the program pulled us inside and gave us assignments. I was too embarrassed to say no.

Our instructions were simple: These are our guests; welcome them with a smile; serve them all they want to eat; keep their glass full and their plate full; and offer to fill any containers they brought. Easy.

There was nothing sanitized about this experience. The majority of our guests were homeless men, many were in need of baths and clean clothes, almost all were exceedingly polite and grateful, and each one was living on the streets and hoping to have a bed and a shower when the shelter opened later that day. I understood my job and my limitations. I would offer water or juice, the comfort of a warm meal, and the human connection of eye contact and a smile. I could do this all morning for what seemed to be an endless line of men. And then I found my weakness: a young mother came in with a young child and a toddler.

She was taken to a table that gave her a little bit of privacy, away from the open space, and I welcomed her as I had welcomed the others. I tried to meet her eyes, but they were downcast. The children were very quiet, very well-behaved, and I entertained them with coloring pages. We brought them their food, which they ate quickly and in silence. I packed some extra sandwiches in their bag. The policy was to provide soup or sandwiches, but not both. I broke the rules, and I got caught by one of the workers, who looked at me with such compassion that I felt more exposed than I've ever felt in my life. I ended the day hiding in the bathroom in tears.

I cherish that experience both for the opportunity to have served the hungry on that day, but also for the self-discovery that I must empty myself in order to truly serve. I learned that the powerful impact of service is not done for a group, but for the person, seeing the inherent goodness and dignity of persons individually, rather than reducing them to a subset of society.

Perhaps this is the supernatural power that God gives to saints such as Mother Teresa of Calcutta or Marianne Cope. They can empty themselves totally and become vessels for God's love. How else could they serve the poor and destitute of India, as Mother Teresa did so beautifully, or tend to the sick and suffering in Hawaii's leper colonies, as St. Marianne Cope did? These saints showcase the diverse ways women contribute to the well-being of others. They took dramatic shifts in their life's work, demonstrating that a Second Act can often prove to be the catalyst for truly finding oneself.

Mother Teresa: Mother to "the Least of These"

Anjeze Gonxhe Bojaxhiu was born on August 26, 1910, in Skopje, North Macedonia. Her father was a successful businessman, and her mother instilled in her and her brother and sister a strong sense of compassion and charity. When their father died, their mother continued to raise them in a deeply religious and loving home. Anjeze's mother must have been a model of motherhood that Mother Teresa carried into the streets of Calcutta.

When Anjeze turned eighteen, she left home and joined the Sisters of Loreto in Ireland. She took the name Sr. Mary Teresa in honor of both the Blessed Mother and Thérèse of Lisieux. Then, in 1929, Sr. Teresa was assigned to teach school at St. Mary's School for Girls in Calcutta, India. She taught there for twenty years, eventually becoming principal of the school.

I'm always surprised to discover how many saints, both female and male, have been teachers at some point in their lives. It shouldn't surprise me; in fact, it encourages me to look deeper within myself to keep working on those virtues that led to a career in education for me. Sr. Teresa was instructed in the virtues of compassion and charity. Of course, it makes sense that she would teach, as children need both compassion and love in order to thrive in an educational setting, and in life.

Sr. Teresa's life seemed to be on a good trajectory, and I'm sure she felt a sense of purpose and fulfillment in both teaching and leadership, but that changed rather suddenly. Having taken her final profession and settled into what she believed to be her life, the now *Mother* Teresa committed herself fully to the sisters, and to a life of poverty, chastity, and obedience. Sometimes a Second Act develops slowly over time and we have the opportunity to ponder and even plan for the changes that are coming. Not Mother Teresa. Her Second Act came on suddenly while traveling on a train to Darjeeling for a retreat. She received a mystical vision of Christ, and it changed her heart immediately. In this vision, Christ spoke to her from the cross, saying, "I thirst." Mother Teresa understood that he wanted her to take care of "the least" of his children, the poor that were marginalized, unseen, uncared for. Mother Teresa accepted the invitation from her Lord, calling it a "call within a call." She returned to the convent convicted and determined to respond fully to Christ's call.

Mother Teresa's Second Act

With the permission of her superiors, Mother Teresa left the Sisters of Loreto to enter her new mission field, working directly with the poor in the slums of Calcutta. Just two years later, in 1948, she attained Indian citizenship and began her work with the poor. Now unaffiliated with the Sisters of Loreto, she put on a simple white sari with a blue border and went to work.

The Vatican granted Mother Teresa permission to start the Missionaries of Charity in 1950. The order started small, with a few local women, but it grew quickly as word spread. It was not long before the Missionaries of Charity were known around the world, garnering attention from heads of state and international organizations, and most notably, from St. John Paul II. As women around the world were inspired to join her order, the Missionaries of Charity expanded their reach and their services. They provided free services to the poor, ran homes for the dying, operated dispensaries and clinics, and opened soup kitchens and counseling centers. They also ran schools and orphanages. Everywhere they went, they took care of "the least" among them.

Mother Teresa remained at the forefront of the action. It would have been easy for her to step back into an administrative role, but she served the poor in a very physical way, often literally picking them up off the streets and carrying them home, to die with dignity and surrounded by others who loved in equal measure. Mother Teresa did the work she expected from others. She also had a quick wit that didn't give people a pass. Once, at a reception with wealthy donors and celebrities, Mother Teresa was approached by a gentleman who, having engaged her, took out his checkbook and wrote a $10,000 donation to the Missionaries of Charity. Mother Teresa gave him back his check, telling him she didn't want his money, she wanted him. I bet that shook him, but he took her at her word and volunteered at one of her homes for the poor. I'm sure she still got the money, but the bigger scope of her response was in having the man understand that he, too, was called to serve the poor by being the hands and feet of Christ.

Mother Teresa died on September 5, 1997, at the age of eighty-seven. She was beatified by St. John Paul II in 2003, and then canonized in 2016 by Pope Francis. Her legacy is strong with the continued work of the Missionaries of Charity, but what I carry with me the most in her example is to be true to one's mission, as she continued to do the work that she expected of others.

Mother Teresa's work transformed lives; she transformed people, one person at a time, with attention to the individual, with dignity, respect, and love.

Mother Teresa had an extraordinary gift of teaching by example. She modeled unconditional love and service. In the secular world, that kind of leadership is called mentoring, and perhaps to a large degree it is, as certainly her sisters and volunteers would have learned by working alongside her. However, it was more than that. What I see in Mother Teresa is a spiritual mother I can emulate.

I may not travel into the poorest of the poor places, but I am in the world. Mother Teresa teaches me that I can move through the streets and hallways in my small part of the world with motherly care and compassion, unconditional love, and an eye for spiritual as well as physical nurturing. I find in St. Marianne Cope a kindred spirit who, after a life of teaching nurses and other professionals in the medical arts the importance of leading with compassion, entered her Second Act in the leper colony of Hawaii with self-sacrifice and dedication.

St. Marianne Cope: Paragon of Selfless Service and Compassion

St. Marianne Cope was born Barbara Koob on January 23, 1838, in Heppenheim, Germany. She emigrated with her family to Utica, New York, when she was a year old. In her twenties, when her father became ill, Barbara went to work in the local textile factory to help support the family.

When her father died in 1862, Barbara felt the freedom to pursue her calling to the religious life, and joined the Sisters of St. Francis in Syracuse, New York. The following year, as Sr. Marianne, she received the habit of the Sisters of the Third Order Regular of St. Francis, and again, as I learned to my surprise and joy, she became a teacher, and then a principal. I love this so much! As a German immigrant, she taught German-speaking children in those schools. It is so important for children to see themselves in their teachers, and she must have been a wonderful gift to the children and their families.

Sr. Marianne's success as principal primed her for other leadership positions in her community. Within her order, she served in various administrative positions, and then went on to serve as one of the founding members of St. Joseph's Hospital in Syracuse, one of the first public hospitals in the country. The hospital's mission was to serve anyone who needed medical care regardless of their race, creed, or ability to pay. This attitude of inclusion and compassion would be a hallmark of the rest of her life.

The hospital's model of success carried into other aspects of its administration, including revolutionary changes in healthcare education. Sr. Marianne was instrumental in the opening of St. Elizabeth's Hospital in Utica, which was a trailblazer in establishing a school of nursing in the hospital setting. She believed that compassion was an integral part of the nursing profession; thus she stayed close to the training process to maintain quality control. This approach would become an essential part of the profession for generations to come.

Sr. Marianne's far-reaching approach to hospital administration and healthcare education helped lead the hospitals in New York to renown. Her leadership and compassion came to the attention of King Kalakaua of Hawaii, possibly through diplomatic channels. In 1883, he reached out to Sr. Marianne, asking her if she would provide assistance in managing hospitals in Hawaii. Many people were suffering from Hansen's disease and had been isolated to prevent the spread of leprosy. Ten years earlier, St. Damian had begun his work as administrator of the leper colony at Kalaupapa (on the island of Molokai), but there was great need for the sisters to serve as nurses elsewhere on the islands. As frightening as this disease was at the time, Sr. Marianne and a missionary team of six sisters responded to the king's request, and they went to Honolulu that very same year, opening a sacrificial Second Act.

The Sisters' Second Act

Upon their arrival in Hawaii, the sisters immediately set to work. Sr. Marianne managed the Kaka'ako Branch Hospital where her brand of compassionate care and administrative efficiency caught on. In 1889, in the final days of St. Damian of Molokai, Sr. Marianne and her sisters went to continue the administration of the medical care there, and lovingly served their spiritual and other needs. Before leaving for this new assignment, Sr. Marianne assured her sisters that God would protect them from illness, and no one ever became ill. Sr. Marianne continued Fr. Damian's mission on Kalaupapa, committing herself not only to serving the people's medical needs but also improving their living conditions.

Like Mother Teresa, who served vast numbers of poor people by serving them individually, one at a time, Sr. Marianne approached her care one patient at a time. After noticing that a little girl living in the settlement had become withdrawn, despairing over the physical and emotional pain of her illness, Sr. Marianne took a special interest in her. She often sought out the child to bring her out of her shell. First, she simply spent time with her, inviting her to join in small activities. As the girl began to open up, Sr. Marianne gave her small tasks to complete, until eventually, the girl felt a sense of purpose and belonging. On her birthday, Sr.

Marianne threw a little party for her, changing the girl's outlook and giving her a new appreciation for life despite her illness.

This kind of care, a focus on the dignity of each person, had a profound effect on those she served in Molokai.

Sr. Marianne never returned to New York. She lived the rest of her life on Molokai, like St. Damien, serving "the least" around her. Sr. Marianne's legacy of empathy and compassion became a beacon of hope for those served by her and the other sisters. She is remembered for her pioneering healthcare policies and administration, but more so for her devoted service to the people of Hawaii.

QUESTIONS TO PONDER

1. Have you ever had to step out in faith to do something that was frightening or scary?

2. How were St. Teresa of Calcutta and St. Marianne Cope "mothers" to those they served?

3. How do our relationships with our mothers, mother figures, spiritual mothers, or the Blessed Mother inform our approach to service?

CHAPTER 5

Extraordinary Artists

Creatives Who Made the World Better

"We are marching towards home, the holy city. The spiritual journey is the journey home. Everybody knows where home is. Home is where you're loved."
　　　　　　　　　　　　–Servant of God Thea Bowman[1]

When I was a very little girl, my parents said I would take the *TV Guide*, which listed the television shows for the week, and look for a particular art school advertisement that had a cartoon image. The ad encouraged you to draw the image and send it in for evaluation. I'm sure it was a scam, and everyone who submitted a drawing sample was encouraged to take this art school correspondence course for a price, but I never tried to send in my work. The images changed from week to week, and I would sit for hours, diligently working on my art project. To encourage me, my parents bought me a beginner's set of acrylic paints, some small canvases and brushes, and a step-by-step art book for painting landscapes.

I loved my gift! I would spend many Saturday afternoons following directions for creating clouds that looked like real clouds instead of puffs of cotton candy, and trees that had leaves instead of a bubble of green. Eventually, I entered some art shows at school, and even had some success with my nature pieces.

Then, one day, I put away my painting and picked up a pen. My imagination ran wild with stories, and for the next decade, my afternoons were spent creating characters that peopled new worlds. Occasionally, when the teenage angst would hit, I'd write dozens of trite poems. I rarely shared those stories and poems, but I did spend lots of time working on and developing my writing. It was time well spent, just as the afternoon basketball practices made me a better player.

I continued to write fiction well into college until, emboldened by encouragement from my friends, I started to submit my work to magazines. In those days, it was quite an ordeal to submit anything for publication. It involved including a self-addressed envelope with a stamp so the editors could contact you. I spent a lot of change on stamps, and I grew to hate my handwriting when I would see my hand-addressed envelope return to me with a small strip of blue or yellow paper inside that said "Thanks, but no thanks."

Eventually, I quit sending my work out for consideration. I had gotten married and was working as a technical writer for the Department of Defense. After that, I spent the next thirty or so years of my life teaching writing. Did I miss writing fiction and poetry? Sometimes. Mostly, I was a busy wife and mother, with little time to write in the evenings after long days of teaching.

Although I did occasionally draw pictures for my children and create little storybooks for them over summer breaks.

As my children grew up and found their interests and activities, I discovered blogging. It seems that everyone I knew in the early 2000s had a blog, and I dared to jump into the deep end and start my own blog. At first, it was a silly place to put my wild ideas and unchecked opinions (I don't think much has changed on the internet and social media). I was encouraged to write in this space, and especially enjoyed that people liked what I was writing, too. It was a complementary activity with the work I was doing in the classroom. So much so, that I incorporated blogging for my students as projects to have their writing published for others to read.

In all this time, I never once considered myself an artist. I would occasionally pick up a pencil and doodle, or draft a short poem that was more aspiration than cohesive thought, and I wrote regularly on my blog. I even picked up a new hobby: photography. Digital photography made it easier for me to practice getting the right shot. It went nicely with blogging, and I was content to keep on as I had.

By now, though, I was in my forties. My children were grown and off to college and beyond, and I found myself thinking about retirement. Oh, I know it was a little early for that still, but I was giving some serious thought to the next stage of my life. I would be teaching for many more years, but perhaps I could return to my lifelong dream of writing. I also experienced a profound reversion to the Catholic faith, which led to a stronger Catholic presence online.

I was particularly drawn to a few online Catholic resources, and my interactions there resulted in invitations to write for them. I was over the moon and took these opportunities seriously, determined to use my gifts for God as my devotional life grew stronger.

Over time, I came to appreciate how God uses all our experiences, especially if they seem disconnected or not exactly linear. My early years exploring writing, the decades dedicated to the art of communication in the classroom, even my sometimes inappropriate or uncharitable forays into blogging, helped me develop the craft and discipline of writing. Even the stacks of rejection letters helped me grow, although it seems counterintuitive. God had given me a gift, and now it was time for me to put it to good use in his vineyard.

What happened over the next decade was nothing short of miraculous. I wrote on Catholic topics close to my heart: the family, my children, works of mercy, books and films. I took all my years of technical writing and applied them to nonfiction writing. I wrote books and articles, led retreats, and was invited to give addresses at conferences. All of this used every experience I had gained throughout my life. Now, as I enter my Second Act and ponder what could be the next thing I dedicate myself to, I know that it will be, once again, a kind of re-sorting of my skill set to grow in a new direction for the glory of God.

Like me, the women in this chapter experienced an opportunity to grow beyond the skill set they were comfortable with. I found great inspiration in Grandma Moses. The physical limitations caused by advanced arthritis drove Grandma Moses to find a workaround to the health crisis that curtailed her quilting, demonstrating a creative drive despite challenges of age-related limitations. No longer able to handle the needle for quilting and embroidery, she took up painting at the age of seventy-eight, culminating in a magnificent Second Act filled with remarkable artwork.

Her story speaks to me; I'm barely into my sixties, suffering both from arthritis and Dupuytren's contracture, finding it harder and harder to type. I am unafraid to look for other creative outlets—for example and surprisingly, as an editor helping other writers reach their potential. Servant of God Thea Bowman saw the absence of representation in her religious community and the wider scope of the Catholic Church, and worked to fill that void. She began publishing in her forties and continued to be a voice for the African American experience in the Church, as well as society. Her creative and advocacy work continued right up to her death from breast cancer at the age of fifty-two. She inspires me to keep looking for ways to grow and contribute to God's beautiful world.

Grandma Moses: From Farm Girl to Folk Icon

Anna Mary Robertson was born on September 7, 1860, in Greenwich, in upstate New York, near Vermont. The rural setting was a backdrop that would influence her in years to come. As a farm girl, her days were filled with chores and learning the skills she would need as an adult. Her education was nominal, and typical of the times. By the time Anna was twelve, she had left home to work in private homes. It opened up to her the world beyond the farm.

Anna married Thomas Moses when she was twenty-seven years old. The couple had ten children but only five survived. The life of a tenant farmer was hard, and yet Anna found time to express her creativity using odds and ends on the farm. As a little girl, she was known to cultivate her creativity by using twigs and natural juices from berries and fruit to create colors and designs. Although sewing was a survival skill on the farm, she expanded that skillset to include embroidery. Her talent was well known in her community, and many of her early quilts and embroidery still exist today on exhibit at the Bennington Museum in Vermont.

By 1905, Anna and her husband moved to Eagle Bridge in New York. There, she dedicated herself to the work on the farm, tending to the family, various farm chores, and the delicate embroidery that she became known for locally. While most of the information we have about Anna begins at the age of seventy-eight when her paintings started to garner attention, I am most taken with her nascent feminism despite living a rather traditional life on a farm. In 1952, at the age of ninety-two, she published her autobiography, *My Life's History*. In it, she confesses she found her role as a woman a bit stifling, "Many a time I had to rock the cradle; I liked it, but I had rather been outdoors with my brothers."

I was taken with this woman, who did what was expected of her and fulfilled her obligations to her family and the farm and yet still breathed freely and allowed herself to think beyond the restrictions placed upon her by society. In this brief statement, I found a kindred spirit. I, too, have loved my family, adored being a wife and mother, and also, perhaps in quiet moments, looked forward to a time when I could do something else, perhaps set aside my responsibilities and escape to a little play. In an otherwise austere and little-known life, Anna has become a role model for persevering in her duties and being rewarded for it with a grand Second Act.

Anna's Second Act: Becoming an Icon at Eighty

By the time Anna was in her late seventies, arthritis had ravaged her hands, making it difficult for her to continue embroidery. I can't imagine how devastating it must have felt to have a lifelong skill taken away, and yet I am starting to feel my own limitations from hardening tendons due to illness. Her creative spirit found a new outlet: painting. At her sister's insistence, Anna took up the brush, but it wasn't quite as easy as that. She lacked the resources for proper painter's supplies, so in her early days of painting, in her eighties, she used whatever she could find. Matchsticks became brushes, and whatever household paint she found would do. Her early paintings mostly captured her childhood memories on the family farm.

By then, Anna, a grandmother and great-grandmother many times over, was referred to by the neighbors as Grandma Moses. She gave away many of her paintings, and some local stores sold some of her works. There was something charming in her primitive style. She was self-taught, and loved vibrant colors that captured a certain joyful atmosphere. In addition to depicting scenes from her rural experience, Grandma Moses also made paintings of the seasons, going so far as to add glitter to snow scenes in order to capture the sparkle of the snow. At eighty years old, Grandma Moses could add whatever she wanted to her paintings. I am reminded of the young woman rocking the baby and yearning to be outside playing with her brothers. *You go, girl! Sprinkle glitter on all the things!*

My interest in Grandma Moses stemmed from the fascination that after living a full life, she took on a new hobby, effectively beginning all over again in a new field. I've had some false starts and shifts at work that took me to unexpected places, but I've never pondered the possibility of setting aside my writing and picking up a paintbrush to start all over again at seventy-eight years old. And why not? I could take up the piano, or do ballroom dancing, or . . . or . . . or. Grandma Moses has taught me that the only one keeping me from taking on new things *right now* is me.

Grandma Moses's catapult to fame happened quite by accident. In 1938, an art collector named Louis Caldor happened upon some of her work in a drugstore in Hoosick, New York. He was so taken with it that he bought out the store and went on a quest to find more of her pieces. In 1940 he introduced her to the world with an exhibit of her artwork in a show called "What a Farm Wife Painted." I'm not sure how I feel about the title. Was he trying to capture his surprise at encountering these works or did it play to the humble origins of the artist? Accounts suggest he was truly enthralled by the simplicity of her compositions, and the point of view either from above or far away in order to capture all the details included in the paintings. Her untrained hand created charming snapshots of a bygone era, and the public was thrilled to have the simplicity of those days captured in her art.

Few painters are as prolific as Grandma Moses, who painted more than 1500 pieces in a twenty-year period. Her fame was as much about her *attitude* toward work as it was about the work itself. Years ago, when I was thinking about what I would like to do when I retired, I ran across a quote in a social media post attributed to Grandma Moses: "If I hadn't started painting, I would have raised chickens." Maybe she said it, maybe she didn't, but it certainly speaks to an attitude of productivity. At eighty, she was still vibrant, still very much interested in her world. To me, her art not only represents a beautiful era but also a beautiful woman who found joy in the everyday simplicity of living. I might giggle at the thought of a little old lady spreading glitter gleefully on a snow scene, but only because her joy is contagious.

Servant of God Thea Bowman, FSPA

Another artist who lived in the twentieth century, Sr. Thea Bowman, moved me with her energy, spirit-filled song, and joyful expression of the Gospel. As we begin to encounter more and more saints-in-the-making from the twentieth century, we have access to more than their writings; we have the opportunity to listen to their words and watch them in action through archived videos accessible to all. Servant of God Thea Bowman is one such holy woman. To watch her in action is to be evangelized, to be touched by the fire in her soul.

I discovered Sr. Thea shortly after the cause for her canonization was opened in 2018. I was living in south Alabama in a Black Creole community not too far from Mississippi. There was great excitement in the Mobile area, and I followed the news stories about her. I've always loved writing about the saints, and I was always looking for a connection with them. In Sr. Thea, I found a connection immediately: she was a teacher as well as an artist.

Sr. Thea was born Bertha Bowman in Yazoo City, Mississippi, in 1937. Her father was a medical doctor and her mother was a teacher. Her family moved to Canton, where she grew up surrounded by a loving community. As a Black woman growing up in the segregated Deep South, the young Bertha was no stranger to racism and inequality. She immersed herself in her community and culture, learning from the elders and absorbing the culture. It formed her identity early on, particularly after her conversion, as a Black Catholic. All her gifts of self-expression—in word, spirituality, and song—flowed from that rock-solid sense of identity in an enduring legacy of faith.

Bertha was not raised Catholic, although she had a deep spiritual upbringing and loved attending church to learn and sing. A precocious child, her parents sent her to the Catholic school that served Black children in their town, Holy Child Jesus School. There, she was taught by the Franciscan Sisters of Perpetual Adoration. They would be her destiny, as she shared with her parents at age nine that she wanted to become Catholic, and at fifteen that she wanted to join the FSPA order. Institutional racism ran through much of the Catholic Church in the United States, and it was unusual for religious orders to accept postulants of color. Nevertheless, Bertha embarked on the trip to La Crosse, Wisconsin, where she joined the order.

She excelled in her studies and after several years was a professed sister. Taking the name Sr. Mary Thea in honor of the Blessed Mother and her father, Theon, Sr. Thea embarked on what would be a beautiful career in education. Within a few years, she was reassigned to her childhood school in Canton, where she returned to teach within her own community. I had that in common with Sr. Thea, as I taught in the high school I had attended. There's a special joy in that, when the students who look like you and have the same background see what they can become.

I've always thought that teaching was a kind of performance art. Watching Sr. Thea teach and speak confirms this, as she is not just animated but likely to launch into song to illustrate her point. She was educated at Viterbo College with a degree in English, speech, and drama, and earned her PhD from Catholic University of America (CUA) in English literature and linguistics. She went on to teach at CUA, Viterbo, and Xavier University in New Orleans. I love that everything she did was about educating people.

I could go on and on about Sr. Thea's teaching and speaking career, and I maintain it is a form of art to know how to reach an audience and communicate straight into their hearts, but Sr. Thea's use of music in those presentations merit mentioning. She believed the universal language of music would touch hearts deeply, and she was not shy about incorporating song into her presentations. Her voice was powerful, rich, and a pleasure to hear.

Sr. Thea's Second Act

When Sr. Thea was diagnosed with cancer in 1984, she entered into a Second Act that was not covered in sorrow or anxiety but rather was filled with joy and faith. She traveled across the country giving speeches and presentations that shared African American culture with Catholic teachings. Her evangelization resonated with inclusion, encouraging the Church to embrace diversity. She became an ardent advocate for empowering individuals and communities.

Sr. Thea's testimony of joy and suffering spoke to the redemptive power of suffering. She spoke candidly about her illness, maintaining a joyful demeanor filled with song, and an unwavering faith that uplifted and inspired everyone around her.

In 1989, Sr. Thea addressed the United States Conference of Catholic Bishops for the Subcommittee on African American Affairs. She opened with a compelling question, "What does it mean to be Black in the Church in society?" And then she launched into a beautiful and haunting Black spiritual:

> Sometimes I feel like a motherless child,
> Sometimes I feel like a motherless child,
> Sometimes I feel like a motherless child,
> A long way from home, a long way from my home.
> Sometimes I feel like an eagle in the air,
> Sometimes I feel like an eagle in the air,
> Sometimes I feel like an eagle in the air,
> Still. I'm a long way, I'm a long way, I'm a long way.[2]

I gasped at the depth of meaning in her opening, an opening far more effective than if she had merely explained her feelings. To be sure, the Black bishops must have been affected by this answer to the question, but Sr. Thea probably banked on the universality of music to carry her point to every corner of the room. The pain of isolation coupled with the exhilaration of soaring as an eagle does not take away from the reality that there is work to be done and progress still to be made.

Sr. Thea traveled extensively to give workshops and lectures, and used music and storytelling to illustrate her points. I imagine that she taught in the fashion of griots, West African storytellers who kept the history and traditions of their people alive through their performances. In many ways, Sr. Thea did this, bringing African American culture into the worship space. She emphasized the importance of being a "fully functional" member of the Church, being authentically herself, authentically African American, and authentically Catholic. Those identities are all of a piece, and she wanted African Americans to be able to enjoy this fullness in the Church.

To this end, Sr. Thea contributed to the creation of a uniquely African American Catholic hymnal called *Lead Me, Guide Me,* which was published in 1987. The hymnal embraces the contributions of African Americans to the spiritual life of the Church in America. It celebrates the tradition of spiritual and gospel music in the Black experience, and infuses the Mass with a more inclusive and joyful welcome for all, especially the Black members who find their tradition a part of the liturgy.

Sadly, Sr. Thea died of breast cancer in 1990 at just fifty-two years old, months after that powerful address to the US bishops. Knowing she was dying, she launched herself into an early Second Act in a whirlwind of public speaking to realize this goal of encouraging both African Americans and the Church to come together in a fully functional way. Her tombstone says, simply, "I tried."

Although Sr. Thea is remembered for her racial justice and her advocacy for cultural inclusion, I like to think of her as the consummate artist, a brilliant evangelist.

QUESTIONS TO PONDER

1. What kind of artistic expression would you most like to pursue as part of your Second Act? Perhaps learn to play an instrument, take up photography, or join a literary or writer's group?

2. Grandma Moses responded to the loss of her ability to continue to pursue her love of embroidery by finding a suitable, adjacent artistic expression. What role do hobbies have in your life?

3. Sr. Thea Bowman introduced music into her public speaking. Can you think of a way to share an artistic expression of yourself in the regular work that you do?

CHAPTER 6

Champions of Social Justice

Who Fought to Protect and Improve Lives

"There is no room for contempt of others in the Christian life. To criticize the social order is one thing, people another."

—Servant of God Dorothy Day[1]

When I was in the fourth or fifth grade, I learned a new word: boycott. The early 1970s was a time of great turbulence, and I was on the cusp of young adulthood, listening to the news, listening to my parents and their friends debate issues, and having conversations in and out of the classroom at school. At the time, I thought I was grasping what was going on in the world, but in retrospect, I lacked the maturity and basic knowledge about all that was happening to make sense of it. The Vietnam War was coming to a close, the United States was leading the world in space travel with several missions to the moon, and the Watergate scandal was just hitting the news. Not to mention the hippie movement "love-ins" that disrupted my weekends at the park.

I asked a lot of questions, and when I did get answers, they usually went over my head. I was particularly interested in the United Farm Workers' strike. The UFW represented the farm workers, and efforts to negotiate contracts had already resulted in a grape boycott that led to undocumented Mexican workers coming in as strikebreakers. This topic dominated many of the adult conversations in my home. Immigration, the right to work and receive fair wages, and related topics were at the forefront of most serious conversations at my parents' dinner parties.

And me? I liked grapes and didn't want a boycott. Cesar Chavez was often mentioned at the dinner table, and I remember that there were factions among the adults who supported Chavez's efforts, and just as many who didn't. I didn't understand, but I knew I wanted my grapes and wondered why the powers-that-be couldn't figure it out.

Some fifty years later, I ask myself the same question.

I never did get any resolution on the boycott issue. Right in the middle of all the social and political farm worker drama, the Supreme Court issued the landmark *Roe v. Wade* decision. In an overwhelming 7–2 vote, this decision gave women the right to choose abortion, and protected their choice.

This created quite a shift in the conversations going on around me. In the mid-1970s, feminism had gained serious momentum and the Equal Rights Amendment was gaining traction in a majority of the states. I was a little older, a bit more knowledgeable, and (thanks to my success as an athlete) a lot more combative on and off the basketball court. I wanted to know why the boys got premium practice times, new uniforms, and pep rallies. I looked forward to Billie Jean King whomping Bobby Riggs in the "Battle of the Sexes" tennis match. I applauded Title IX as a victory for girls' sports (which it was).

I emerged from the seventies relatively unscathed by the turbulent social change, and yet in a sense I *was* changed. I entered young adulthood with a profound sense of social justice. I knew what was right and wrong, and I knew what was fair and unfair. Abortion was wrong. Not paying fair wages for work was wrong. Limiting educational and professional opportunities based on the accident of birth was unfair.

Now, of course, I can add dozens of instances of unfair treatment. I wouldn't style myself a social justice warrior, but then again, what's in a name? I celebrated the overturning of *Roe v. Wade* in June of 2022. It truly shocked me, as I never thought I'd see that in my lifetime. Each election in the past twenty or so years has been fraught with controversy and disappointment, and I have decried the outcomes of each new election cycle. I educate myself on the candidates like never before. The subject of immigration, a topic that has been close to my heart literally my entire life, depresses me.

But what happened to the sassy girl who challenged the status quo in the athletic office or volunteered with the service organizations in high school? Somewhere within me is the young woman who left the revolutionary era of the 1970s wanting to change the world. She went to college, pursued her goals, got married, and started a family. I don't blame her—she had to find her place in the world, and she did.

Becoming a teacher sharpened my sense of justice and human dignity. I was drawn to the students who entered the educational game with deficits, recognizing the social and economic inequalities that made success for my students difficult. The educational system was (and still is) failing to level the playing field because the factors that often lead to success are established long before the children start school. Poverty, like wealth, is often passed from one generation to the next, and education doesn't always break the cycle.

While I was teaching high school, I was a cheerleader for my students. In those days, classes were composed of students performing at the same reading and writing levels. My students tended to fall into the category of what today we call "emerging readers and writers." In that era these classes had a pejorative label: "remedial studies." How could I encourage success when these students carried around that stigma on their transcripts? It took a lot of work and a lot of thinking outside the box, but my students succeeded. I'm convinced that I loved them into an education. Was I one hundred percent successful? No. But it was pretty darn close.

When I shifted my career to teaching at the college level, I saw an opportunity for greater influence. I still taught remedial courses, but this time to adults. Adults who either had young children or would possibly have children in their future. I saw an opportunity to facilitate being an agent of change for my adult students to make changes for *their* children before they started school. Although I started teaching college at a small liberal arts university, I shifted to the technical college system, where I think I had the most influence.

My favorite part about teaching at a technical college lies in the hope it offers, especially hope for getting out of poverty. In eighteen months, students can graduate with a technical diploma that allows them to enter the workforce with a well-paying job. Additional training prepares them for greater advances in the workforce. Rather than getting into debt at colleges and universities (and getting caught in overwhelming debt and possibly not finishing), my students sacrificed hard for a short period of time and saw gains. It was truly my favorite job, and I didn't squander the opportunity to extend my influence.

When I was in college, my educational methodology professor taught so exceptionally well that I very rarely took notes. He taught us like we were in kindergarten, with music and pictures, singing and silly antics, and it all stuck to my brain. I asked him why he didn't teach kindergarten, because I admired him so much and thought it would be a wonderful experience for kindergarteners to have him as their teacher. His response informed how I would teach for the rest of my life. He said, "If I teach a kindergarten class, I will impact only twenty-five students in a year. But if I teach four sections of thirty-five future teachers, three times a year, I will impact 420 students who will each teach twenty-five students in a year." I did the math: that's 10,920 students.

I won't go into what that number means over the lifetime of those teachers, because the number is staggering. I *will* say that extending the scope of influence changes lives, and I wanted to change lives. In the writing courses I taught, I had the academic freedom to choose the topics we discussed and wrote about. I had my students set goals, make actionable plans, and think critically about solutions to challenges. We discussed how they could integrate those very topics into their discussions with their children.

As teachers, we never really know the impact we've had on our students. It keeps us humble and continuing to do the good work in the classroom. But I'd like to think that if I helped even one person get out of poverty, then all the late nights planning and grading have been worth the effort. I never saw myself as a champion of social justice, but I was certainly a champion of human dignity, and perhaps that's the same thing.

In this chapter, I look to two courageous and persevering champions of social justice for inspiration: Helen Alvaré and Dorothy Day. Helen Alvaré teaches law at George Mason University and is a prolific writer and speaker on issues of marriage and parenting. Dorothy Day, one of the founders of the Catholic Worker Movement, championed the poor and worked to improve conditions for the working class. I greatly admire Alvaré, whose writings I've often been drawn to, and I had to come to an appreciation for Day, whom I admit, I misunderstood and even rejected for many years because of my own bias. Both women work(ed) for the dignity of the human person, and I feel a kinship with them in my own work as I enter a Second Act in my retirement that returns me to my beginnings working with families in the challenges of poverty and disadvantage.

Helen Alvaré: Champion of Families

I recently had the pleasure of hearing Helen Alvaré speak at the National Catholic Prayer Breakfast in Washington, DC, in February of 2024. She received the Christifidelis Laici Award for her good work in serving the Church. Her charming speech revealed both her humility and fierce dedication to the Catholic faith.

I first heard of Dr. Alvaré when I watched the playback of her address at the ninth annual National Catholic Prayer Breakfast in 2013. I was working in Catholic new media at the time, trying to find my own voice in the Catholic conversation, and was trying to balance writing serious pieces about what was happening in the culture with ridiculous memes and general foolishness on Twitter and elsewhere. I was content with producing spiritual-lite content on my blog, a kind of vague and not Catholic-specific nod to being a good person while avoiding ruffling feathers. Call it cowardice, or maybe laziness. Call it being fearful of saying the wrong thing. In any event, it made my content rather vapid and not at all a source of either encouragement or authenticity.

I happened to watch the playback of the prayer breakfast address by accident. It wasn't what I was looking for, but it was clearly what I needed to hear. Alvaré was a breath of fresh air—funny and serious, charming and erudite. Above all, she is a clear communicator and teacher, so it was easy for me to settle in and listen.

"You live when you live," she told her audience, "in the place where you're put. You're given the issues you're given." I reflected on my writing and how I chose to write about the easy things and not engage in what was going on around me, whether in local situations or the national stage, especially about the Catholic faith.

"You can't choose the needy people you have to serve in order to be a good Christian," she went on to say. "Likewise, I don't think you get to choose which moral and human rights issues you will have to address as a Catholic in order to serve the common good in the era and the place where you've been put." Her words challenged me to the core. My work in education was getting increasingly difficult; policies and social standards were changing faster than I could keep up.

Helen Alvaré's career is a testament to this idea that we must rise to our own occasion and be unafraid in our defense of the vulnerable, and courageous in our expressions of faith. Her resume is extensive and impressive, but I am most struck by her unwavering commitment to the faith in a largely secular setting, demonstrating that we do not have to sacrifice or dilute our values or our faith in order to live in the world.

Alvaré studied law at Cornell Law School, graduating in 1984. She worked in law firms in Philadelphia before moving on to represent the United States Conference of Catholic Bishops (USCCB) as a spokesperson for the Secretariat of Pro-Life Activities. In this position she addressed important issues in the Church regarding abortion, contraception, and the family. This foundational work carried through to her illustrious career in academia, first at the Catholic University of America Columbus School of Law, and then as professor at George Mason University's Antonin Scalia Law School.

It's one thing to speak on Catholic themes while working for the USCCB or CUA, and quite another to be teaching law in a secular institution while publishing and speaking on "Catholic" themes such as the dignity of the human person, the sanctity of life, and the importance of the child and the family. Her gift of presenting complex topics in an accessible way has made her a powerful spokesperson before Congress and in other public forums on issues such as abortion and religious freedom. She cofounded Women Speak for Themselves, an organization empowering women to speak in defense of religious freedom, particularly in areas of their reproductive health (specifically, the insurance mandates requiring payment coverage for treatments and procedures that conflict with one's moral principles).

Unafraid to speak out on controversial topics that threaten the human person and the family unit, Alvaré integrates faith and reason into the public discourse. Her 2012 book, *Breaking Through: Catholic Women Speak for Themselves*, reflects a commitment to the faith even with potentially contentious issues such as the impact of the sexual revolution, the complementarity of men and women, and the protection of children—the focus of her book *Putting*

Children's Interests First in US Family Law and Policy: With Power Comes Responsibility (2017).

Like me, Alvaré has Cuban roots, and we are close in age. Her career has been a steady exercise in perseverance, perhaps demonstrating some shifts according to where she has worked, but always with the same themes surrounding the family. For me, the cruelty and abuses of a Communist regime often surfaced in conversations in my childhood home. It was my earliest understanding that the world is sometimes a violent and unfair place filled with injustice and cruelty. I experienced firsthand what the government-mandated breakup of the family does to a child. Alvaré's advocacy for children and the family encompasses much of her work, directly or indirectly. Seeing her receive the Christifidelis Laici Award was a treat, yet it is her words from that day that stayed with me. In her brief acceptance speech, she offered a "Top Ten" list (in the comic style of David Letterman) titled "Wisdom I've Picked Up While Working for Christ and His Church." The list was, of course, hilarious, but also wise. After some self-deprecating notes about having good hair and a propensity for speeding, she got to item number 4: *Be a true disciple first.*

This is a life principle shared by both Helen Alvaré and Dorothy Day, whom you will meet next. Both these women's lives remind us that any work we do in the vineyard must first be for the Lord. To do the Lord's work, we must be true disciples. This insight became especially important to me as I got to know Dorothy Day, whose association with the Communist Party made her a controversial figure in my upbringing. I had a difficult time reconciling this, until I discovered that Day, too, understood that first, one must be a true disciple.

Dorothy Day, Founder of the Catholic Worker Movement

I never wanted to have anything to do with Dorothy Day. I suspect that there may be many people like me who associate the Catholic Worker movement with communism. As a Cuban immigrant who first came to the United States with firsthand knowledge of the violent nature of communism and its disregard for the human person, its destruction of the family, and its mistrust and antagonism of the Catholic Church—in fact, of any religion—I angrily dismissed Day as yet another misinformed ideologue.

In my mind, she was a communist hiding behind the thin veneer of social justice, and since I am being brutally honest, I lumped anyone who thought she was a hero into the same category. I had no time for such folly.

So why am I including her among so many women that I admire? The first reason is simple: she deserves a spot. Day was, in fact, affiliated with the Socialist Party at some time in her young adult years. And although her journey to holiness may not resonate with me, she inspires many people, as any saint certainly does. In addition, it was her conversion to the Catholic faith that pushed her away from the socialist mindset and toward the establishment of the Catholic Worker movement. Every saint has a past, the saying goes.

Dorothy Day shows us that as we mature, our perspective and worldview can, and probably should, change as our experiences in our lifetimes change us and we grow. This is especially important because, like Day, I am not the same woman I was at twenty, thirty, or forty, and I am not the same woman at sixty that I was at fifty. It's a powerful lesson in life, and an essential one in faith. At its core, my beef with Dorothy Day and the Catholic Worker movement was my perception that they put social justice above all else, especially the essential component of the Catholic faith.

What I learned is that she had a strong commitment to the Eucharist and attended Mass daily, as so many in the movement did. In fact, it was this love of the Eucharist, the source and summit of our faith, that inspired them daily, pursuing the works of mercy. Social justice was the natural work of a spirit that was driven by holiness. Dorothy Day and her colleagues were disciples first, and the rest flowed from that calling.

Dorothy Day is a source of encouragement and inspiration for all of us entering into a Second Act. She might have done quite well to continue on the path she began as a journalist. She might even have been an effective socialist and brought about significant social change because even then, as a young woman, the seeds of the Gospel were deeply ingrained in her actions. Even though she fancied herself a revolutionary, she had the self-awareness to see a disconnect between the ideal and its execution in real time, which often failed.

I judged Dorothy Day before getting to know her and what she actually stood for. I am reminded of Venerable Fulton Sheen's observation that there are many who hate the Catholic Church for what they think it is, but not that many for what it is. Busted. Or at least, convicted. After all, don't we want to be judged by how we finish?

Dorothy Day certainly finished strong. Her beginning was less so, but it was a demonstration of perseverance and grit.

Dorothy Day: A Woman of Humble Beginnings

Dorothy was born in Brooklyn, New York, in 1897. She was one of five children, the daughter of a homemaker mother and a journalist father. His job took them all over the United States. It was in this kind of nomadic lifestyle that Dorothy encountered instances of deep poverty and injustice. It would inform her outlook for the rest of her life.

Like her father, Dorothy moved into journalism. She was influenced by writers in the early part of the twentieth century who wrote about the injustices and atrocities in the factories, and Dorothy developed an affinity for the working class that led to her affiliation with the Socialist Party while attending college at the University of Illinois Urbana-Champaign. She wrote for socialist newspapers, focusing on the plight of the worker. She lived a nomadic lifestyle, too, moving from place to place and finally settling down with two socialist newspapers, *The Masses* and *The Call*.

Her twenties were a time of turmoil as she struggled with her writing, as her concern for working conditions intensified her quest for social justice, and as she felt the very early nudgings of searching for greater meaning in her life. Although she wasn't yet disenchanted with the inconsistencies in socialism, she was starting to see that it was problematic. As she worked closely with the poor, she started to see instances of people expecting goods but not contributing to the community. Still, she continued to not only write for these publications but also consort with leaders in the socialist and communist movements. She admitted later that it was an unfortunate circumstance, but their ideals, if not their practice, happened to align with hers.

Back in New York, Dorothy discovered Catholicism and flirted a little with the idea of faith. Well into the post–World War I era, Dorothy embraced the idea of living in community. She moved to the seashore with some close friends and lived a quiet life for some time, still associating with unionizers and others, no longer calling herself a socialist but continuing to have a heart for the injustices faced by workers seeking fair compensation and humane work conditions.

At about this time, Day experienced a series of broken relationships, including a love affair that resulted in an unexpected pregnancy and the subsequent birth of her daughter. Day's lover did not want children. This was further complicated by an encounter she had with a nun who helped her get the child baptized. The father, a professed atheist, did not stand in the way of the baptism, but in the course of the preparations for it, Day presented herself for baptism and entry into the Catholic Church.

Her conversion changed everything. She parted ways with her lover, instead dedicating herself in equal parts to raising her daughter and developing opportunities to serve the working poor. A collaboration with a French Catholic philosopher, Peter Maurin, who shared many of her ideas, led to the founding of houses (really, in many cases, farms) where workers could find shelter and community.

Day and Maurin started the Catholic Worker Movement and their newspaper by the same name. The most surprising thing I learned is that these workers in the Catholic Worker Movement were daily communicants. They attended daily Mass before heading out to do their work. In both theory and practice, they were disciples of Christ first. They believed firmly in the works of mercy, and yet, they did not put those works ahead of their faith.

These communities were sometimes successful, and just as often abject failures when human nature came to the forefront. It is this failing that I often heard my parents discuss. "Socialism looks appealing on paper," they would say, "but when people get involved, some are truly altruistic and others are in it for what they can get." Day's efforts often came up in conversations about Cesar Chavez. In those early childhood experiences I lacked the maturity to understand, but I did grasp a level of disdain, or at the very least a dismissive air that her brand of social justice was ineffective.

I understand that my parents may have had a knee-jerk reaction to her because of their experiences during the communist revolution, and I also understand that my own bias was colored by this, and yet, my parents also instilled a sense of social justice in me. Advocating for the poor, the marginalized, and the most vulnerable in society is a deeply Catholic endeavor. It is a deeply human endeavor, and both of these women, Helen Alvaré and Dorothy Day, used their writing and influence to bring these important topics into the public discourse.

Their perseverance in making this their life's work is an encouragement to me, and to all of us, reminding us that even if we have missed an opportunity earlier in our lives, we can pick up the standard today. For me, it is an exciting component of this new season of my life. As Alvaré suggests, "I am here, in this time and place. As a disciple of Christ, I must see the work that is before me, and act."

QUESTIONS TO PONDER

1. How can we leverage our compassion and our skill set to aid the marginalized with effective social change?

2. What personal sacrifices is God calling you to make for the sake of social justice? How does faith factor into this?

3. Are you prepared to be a disciple first? What does that mean to you? How will you incorporate this into your Second Act?

CHAPTER 7

Unexpected Trailblazers

Who Found Courage
to Explore New Paths

"Procura obras grandes como Dios y para Dios." (Seek
great works like God, and for God.)

– Mama Antula[1]

Sometimes we think our lives are going to go in one direction, so
we carefully plan. We set goals. We proceed with confidence that
we will be successful.

Then, something happens. It can be a catastrophic loss, a
reversal in fortune, or something positive such as a windfall or an
exceptional opportunity that ushers in a dramatic change in the
direction we thought life was taking us.

For example, as a young woman, I had big dreams of becoming
a writer. I took my cues for what such a life could look like from
every TV show or film showing an impoverished writer tethered

to an antique typewriter with a glass of whiskey, a muse that is as ineffective as they come.

When the time came to choose the path I would follow in adulthood, however, I deferred a dream of writing in favor of steady income. I chose to pursue teaching to help support our growing family. And then, when the children were mostly launched, my husband was diagnosed with a devastating illness. We had to pivot.

I had to pivot. It wasn't the Second Act I was looking forward to, but somehow the hand of God was in it. Has always been in it.

The women who inspired me in this chapter also had to pivot hard. Dolores Hart was making it big in Hollywood when she responded to God's call for the life of a cloistered nun. Maria Antonia de Paz y Figueroa, an eighteenth-century consecrated laywoman in what is now Argentina, rebelled against her family's wishes for her to marry, and ended up founding a spiritual movement. Dolores famously kissed Elvis Presley on the silver screen. Maria Antonia took off at the age of fifteen after angrily telling her father that she refused to get married or become a nun.

And me? I quit my job the moment I was vested in the pension and moved to the Gulf Coast to pursue new adventures. Happily, when I finally did become a writer, the reality of the writer's life was somewhat different from what I'd imagined: my writing space was updated to a laptop, and my muse was a cup of coffee as I enjoyed a beautiful sunrise over Mobile Bay. And yet, we were happily settled—and in so many ways, my God-given dreams did come true in this, my Second Act.

In between the image of the suffering artist and the happy author were decades of hard work as an educator. I didn't actively choose education as a vocation, but rather, it chose me over and over in circumstances that placed me in the role of teacher. I came to this career kicking and screaming, each time professing it was only a temporary assignment. Thirty-five years later, I finally retired from teaching English and composition after stints teaching in high school, followed by a liberal arts university, and then a technical college.

I reconciled myself to that work all those years with this quote: "God knew you before you were born. He has given you certain gifts and talents to develop as you grow in His grace. Feed His lambs with words of wisdom. Light the path for others and God will delight in you. Heavenly Father, help me to fulfill my potential. Give me the grace to overcome my selfishness."[2] I happily gave my gift with words to my students, and found fulfillment along with my sense of purpose.

Each of my teaching assignments carried a large load of technical writing, and yet I always identified myself as an educator, not a writer. I never thought to use the word "and," denoting that I was a teacher *and* a writer.

I never gave up on my dream of writing the Great American Novel, but I did come to terms with my identity as a teacher. I was good at it. I came to not only enjoy it, but to derive great satisfaction from the joys and the challenges of this profession. I came to believe that this was what God wanted for me, and the more I threw myself into this work, the more rewarding it became.

After all those years, quitting became difficult, but the timing—God's timing—was perfect. I had just published my first book, and my husband and I were pursuing a dream to move to the Gulf Coast. I tendered my resignation and found myself unemployed in a new city. In the years since, I've often used the word *retired* to describe my circumstances. My identity had been so tied to my job as an educator that not teaching meant I was retired, but I didn't immediately see that I was still working as a teacher, of sorts.

I explored more writing as well as retreat-leading and speaking. I offered spiritual encouragement in workshops. I even took on the challenge of mentoring a couple of writers. I did this all with a measure of joy beyond anything I'd done before, and realize now that it was because I did it for the kingdom of God.

What I didn't recognize right away was the obvious: I was teaching. I was no longer in a classroom, but I was teaching nonetheless. This was a hard realization for me. I resisted the label of teacher for several decades. In fact, it took my quitting education to finally own the title of teacher, and even that still carries a caveat. I like to quote Maya Angelou when asked about how she identifies herself: "I am a teacher who writes."

In the end, it is the best of both worlds for me. It took some spiritual maturity for me to realize that my strength and success came when I stopped resisting my gift of teaching. My surrender to the Lord's will came with a great deal of peace and a surprising number of opportunities for me to use writing in speaking and retreat settings. A new field of work opened up for me that is the intersection of both of those loves.

My Second Act

Retiring from teaching proved to be a new beginning for me rather than the end that I feared. I work as much or as little as I want, enjoy my time with family and friends, and have the satisfaction of seeking the elusive balance in my life that we all aspire to achieve. I don't always hit the mark, but I get it frequently. It is a blessing to be entering this new season of my life with peace and contentment. It comes down to realizing that living my purpose is not an end, but an ongoing gift.

> God has given each of you a gift from his great variety
> of spiritual gifts. Use them well to serve one another.
> (1 Pt 4:10, NLT)

This theme kept coming up in my life: Use your gifts to serve the Lord. After all, he gave them to you.

Dolores Hart: A Kiss Is Just a Kiss

Her unexpected transformation from Hollywood actress to Benedictine nun left many shaking their heads. Dolores had a promising movie career after famously kissing Elvis Presley in their film, *Loving You*, and then starring in several other films with top leading men. Then . . . she entered religious life. I know I'm not alone in finding this quite a pivot to the wholly unexpected. To the casual observer, it is indeed quite a shift in direction.

My generation, especially, assigns a certain mystery to nuns and religious sisters. We came of age in a time when living in the world meant becoming a part of it. Dolores Hart may have been kissing handsome men on the big screen, but she was living a life of deep personal conviction that was at odds with a Hollywood lifestyle. She wanted to find herself in a setting that gave her peace and fulfilled God's plan for her. Framed within the surrender to God's will for her life, Dolores made a choice that was only unexpected if you weren't paying attention.

Dolores had an unconventional childhood. Her parents had a volatile relationship, and her home life lacked stability and a sense of peace. Her parents' tumultuous relationship had a pattern of separation and reconciliation that left Dolores yearning for stability, which her maternal grandmother initially provided. However, by the time Dolores could articulate this desire, her handsome father had abandoned the family to pursue a career in Hollywood and pursue beautiful women with the same zeal.

After her parents separated, Dolores spent her childhood in periods of living alternately with her mother and with her grandmother. Her mother enrolled Dolores in a Catholic school despite her own tepid approach to religion or spirituality. At a young age, Dolores became drawn to the Catholic faith and was given permission to be baptized. Although her mother and grandmother were not Catholic, they supported Dolores in her new faith.

It was with her grandmother that Dolores felt the greatest sense of security, even though it wasn't always the stable environment one would want for a child. Undeniably, love abounded. To Dolores's delight, her creativity was also encouraged, and she developed a love of performing. It was all undisciplined at first, but she started to be cast in roles.

A natural beauty, Dolores exuded the wholesome air of an ingenue that landed her the role opposite the up-and-coming Elvis Presley. They shared her first on-screen kiss—and yet, for Dolores it was all about being the consummate professional. When Elvis asked her out on a date while they were still filming, she suggested they wait until the movie wrapped. He never asked her again.

To the public, she was the object of desire for good-looking leading men. In her private life, she was in a serious relationship that seemed to be pointing toward marriage. Despite working in an industry that was not always compatible with her Catholic values and sensibilities, Dolores maintained her faith and pursued her dreams of a career in acting. And yet, she also felt she was being pulled in another direction.

Casting Calls . . . and God Calling

Dolores made several successful films that poised her for a great career, but she felt a restlessness she couldn't explain. This restlessness took her to New York to pursue the theater. Her talent was undeniable, and she enjoyed a good run in the theater, but the restlessness continued.

A friend suggested that Dolores take some time at a nearby monastery, and thus began her introduction to monastic life at the cloistered Benedictine Abbey of Regina Laudis in Bethlehem, Connecticut. She found great peace there, and returned often, prompting the prioress to ask her what was up with her fascination with the monastery.

Dolores couldn't respond right away, but she had often mused, "My life was not for me."[3] I often felt the same, like things were unfolding before me and I was along for the ride. Unlike Dolores, as a young woman I didn't have the spiritual maturity or understanding of my faith to recognize the power of surrender.

Not Dolores. She was able to hold on to her dream of acting and at the same time recognize a yearning for God, maintaining an open mind and heart to his call.

And so, Dolores had an inkling that perhaps God was calling her to the religious life. She didn't enter the cloister kicking and screaming like I entered education, but she did confess that it was difficult. "A vocation is a call," she reflected, "one you don't necessarily want. The only thing I ever wanted to be was an actress. But I was called by God."[4]

I understand this. Dolores had a career that was taking off and she was starting to see that success in a tangible way. Fan mail overwhelmed her. Unable to keep up with it, she paid her younger brother to take care of responding to requests for signed autographs. Many years later, he ran across a signed photograph with a certificate of authenticity. It was his signature!

Dolores's Second Act: The Convent Calls

If Dolores Hart, the talented actress, brought to life characters on the silver screen, Mother Dolores fully engaged in real life. Most sisters take a new name when they enter the convent. Dolores kept hers, at her mother's request, claiming that Dolores was essential. "You see, Dolorosa, the Mother of Sorrows, bears witness to man's redemption," she explained.[5]

I wonder how an actress-turned-cloistered nun could accomplish this. So did Dolores.

When she finally entered the monastery and spent her first day and night in her new cell, Dolores felt "the enormity" of her decision, and also deep loneliness. "I cried myself to sleep that night. I would cry myself to sleep every night for the next three years."[6]

Dolores had a difficult time reconciling the life she lived as a popular actress with the solitude and isolation of the cloister. She had wanted nothing more than to be an actress, yet she also knew deep down that she was called for something more. It may have been a challenge, but she didn't lose her spirit. Once, in the midst of a difficult time during her novitiate, a visiting friend asked her if there was anything that she wanted or needed. After looking around to make sure that she would not be heard, Dolores whispered, "A vodka martini—very dry."[7]

Astonishingly, Dolores entered the monastery without actually having any idea of what the cloistered life was about. She brought with her a pure desire to answer God's call. It proved beyond challenging. She entered a community that had unwaveringly followed the Rule of St. Benedict for centuries. Dolores was far from a breath of fresh air for the sisters. On the contrary, she experienced a culture shock that might have ended her vocation were it not for a Jesuit priest, Fr. Francis Joseph Prokes, who according to Dolores, challenged the community with the charge of relationship and "awakening that Spirit" when he said he needed to know them not only as a community but as persons. He suggested that the sisters were in denial of their gifts, and insisted that for any women to become a devout religious, "she needed to integrate everything about herself, including what she had done in the world before entering the monastery."[8]

Dolores took this idea of bringing all of herself—including her many gifts—to heart. She had entered the monastery seeking relationship with God, and what she found was a call to love others. Her work at Regina Laudis, whether it was farming, baking, building coffins, or growing into leadership roles that ended in her appointment as prioress, all pointed to relationship.

Dolores had plenty of human struggles in the convent. It's silly to think that people still believe the life of a professed religious is idyllic. One of Dolores's close friends once remarked, "The lady has a temper," and I haven't stopped thinking about it. I have a temper, too, and barely manage it in a small family. I laughed a little when I learned that Dolores once lost it at one of the nuns who was knitting loudly.

Apparently, they were having an important meeting, and the knitting sister was aggressively clicking her needles in annoyance with the direction of the meeting. Dolores yelled at her to knock it off, and then stormed off across the field to cool off. I'm sure it was awkward and embarrassing, but I appreciate her vulnerability in sharing the story. We are all human, all subject to our weaknesses. Her humanity also came out in another anecdote from the cloister. One day there was a din in the common room, and

Dolores was having difficulty getting the attention of the sisters. Harkening back to her childhood, Dolores whistled like a boy. She got her silence, and a few mouths dropping in surprise! I'm sure her presence in the cloister shook things up a little.

My favorite anecdote about Mother Dolores is a little scandalizing. While she was receiving an honorary degree from Fairfield University, the presenter included at the end of the list of her accomplishments the following dubious honor: "She has the distinction of being the only nun in the world whose resume can be found on the website SwingingChicks.com."[9] Instead of being offended, she shrugged sheepishly, further endearing herself to the audience.

Mother Dolores achieved the integration of her professional skills as an actress with her devotion and obedience to God's call for her. The vibrant theater at Regina Laudis is perhaps her great legacy: "The act of consecrating my life—Body and Soul—as a medium for God was a natural extension of my dedication to the media of theater and film as a professional actress. There was no time that I can remember when I didn't want to be an actress, and when I finally did start working in front of the camera, I had the absolute sense of being in a holy place. Holy means belonging to God."[10]

And to think it started with a kiss.

Mama Antula: Feminist and Rebel

Some 250 years ago, at a time when married women had little agency, and religious sisters and nuns had even less, Mama Antula shook up the status quo in eighteenth-century colonial Argentina by refusing to submit to social expectations.

Born to a life of privilege on January 3, 1730, Maria Antonia de Paz y Figueroa possessed a deep spiritual life from childhood, which was nurtured by her parents through her strong education in the Catholic faith. Even as a child, Maria Antonia spent hours in prayer, retiring to her room for spiritual reading and reflection. Otherwise, she would be found in the fields of her father's farm, playing with the Indigenous children and the children of slaves owned by her father. It didn't take Maria Antonia long to realize—and be scandalized by the fact—that her father owned slaves in addition to the indentured workers on his farm.

When Maria Antonia went missing, her parents were often dismayed to discover her learning to cook with the servants or playing barefoot with their children. It often led to violent outbursts from her father, incensed that her mother allowed the girl to wander off barefoot to be among "that kind." Yet it did not deter young Maria Antonia, whose sense of justice and feminist sensibilities had taken root early on.

On occasion, Maria Antonia even challenged her father's prejudiced views and his authoritarian treatment of those in his household. This led to many arguments for the couple—and may have led to Maria Antonia's determination not to marry: she had noticed similar violent and authoritarian propensities in the men in her social circles, and refused to surrender her own agency to such a man.

Maria Antonia was not without suitors, and even fancied one young man enough to make him desserts and a special liqueur that, unbeknownst to her parents, she liked to sample as she was bottling it. In short, Maria Antonia was a normal girl in many ways—except that her eyes were set on the Lord, and she wanted to serve *him*.

Like so many female saints before her, Maria Antonia rebelled against her father's wishes that she marry. She also rejected the idea of entering a monastery. Her objection was simple: she didn't want to be subject to anyone's authority. Instead, she became a *beata*, a consecrated laywoman, and lived in community with other like-minded women. Drawn to Ignatian spirituality, young Maria Antonia left the comfort of her home to pursue a life of sacrifice at the tender age of fifteen.

Maria Antonia joined the work of the Jesuits in colonial Argentina, committed to performing the spiritual exercises developed by St. Ignatius of Loyola. One day she sweetly presented herself to her spiritual director, Fr. Gaspar Suarez, and informed him that she was ready to become a Jesuit and dedicate herself to the missionary life. When he responded that the Jesuits did not admit women, her response was that she would dress in black and consecrate herself. She really wasn't open to having her commitment questioned.

Maria Antonia thought her life would be uneventful, but there was political strife at the time. The Spanish colonies in South America suffered from an identity crisis in being so far from European influence. The Spanish Crown ruled dispassionately from across the world. It was the Jesuits who were a vibrant presence in the daily life of the Americas, operating more than two hundred missions serving 250,000 Indigenous persons. Responsibility for the conversion and education of these souls fell under their purview.

However, in 1767 King Charles III of Spain expelled the Jesuits from Spain and Spanish territories in the Americas, resulting in a redistribution of these missions to other orders or the abandonment of the missions altogether, which was basically the abandonment of the persons being served by the Jesuits. Little is known about what provoked this action, but overnight it became illegal to be a member of the Society of Jesus. Then, in 1773, Pope Clement XIV published a brief of suppression that effectively silenced and removed the Jesuits from their works and influence across the entire Church.

Maria Antonia, now known affectionately by the Quechuan name of Mama Antula (an homage to her maternal affection and a mispronunciation of Antonia), rebelled against this prohibition. Before the suppression of the Jesuits, Mama Antula lived a quiet life in her community of laywomen, caring for the sick and poor within the Viceroyalty of Rio de Plata. It is work that is often left to the women in a community, usually religious sisters or nuns, but in this case to the group of women that Mama Antula joined as a young woman. Under the spiritual guidance of Fr. Gaspar Suarez, she also helped families with instruction for their children. It was an uneventful life, but important for the community. The prohibition against the Jesuits ended that.

Mama Antula's Second Act

Mama Antula could very well have lived out her life in her community and become a saint for the people she served. She came to her service with humility and the desire to do good. However, the same woman who so vehemently rebelled against her father and society's expectations for her now found herself filled with righteous anger and a renewed sense of justice.

This time, Mama Antula's rebellious spirit emboldened her to take on the monumental task of public defiance. The Spanish Crown's prohibition against the Jesuits and the subsequent injunction from the pope may have been a private offense that played out politically, but Mama Antula knew firsthand the impact it would have on the Quechuan people served by the Jesuit missions.

Founding the Confraternity of the Most Blessed Sacrament cemented her newfound purpose to introduce as many people as she could to the teachings of St. Ignatius of Loyola. She was committed to educating the faithful on the Spiritual Exercises, and now more than ever she committed to broadening her reach even if it meant imprisonment or worse.

Mama Antula believed that the practice of the Spiritual Exercises could be an agent of change in a society where poverty and slavery were prevalent. Social change could come, *would* come, with self-reflection on the part of the actors, whether they were governors or governed, slaveholders or slaves. She worked tirelessly to bring all people to God, and did this monumental task through the teaching of the Spiritual Exercises. It was remarkable that she had the support of many priests, and the retreats they organized served hundreds of participants at a time!

Mama Antula's prayer life continued on a path of intimacy with the Lord, always asking what his will was for her and her movement. She consulted with him as with an intimate partner, and thus, when she moved, or as she said, "prayed with action," she did so with great confidence. Her local retreats turned into a national phenomenon, and Mama Antula is credited with being the mother of Argentine spirituality.

Mama Antula's efforts and influence in evangelization and catechesis played a pivotal part in the lives and formation of a country. She picked up a daunting standard when the Jesuits were expelled. However, the part I found most amazing is that she was a prolific letter-writer. In a long-standing tradition of female saints such as St. Catherine of Siena, St. Teresa of Avila, and St. Hildegard of Bingen, her letters to her beloved Jesuits in exile comprised the history of her movement by way of keeping them abreast of her activities. Filled with news and deep spiritual themes of her relationship with God, Mama Antula's letters are a golden nugget in a ministry that took her outside her beloved community and into the countryside and cities of a nascent country—and now, into the world.

QUESTIONS TO PONDER

1. Think of a time in your life when you had to "pivot." What did you learn from that experience? Over time, has it become easier or harder for you to change direction mid-course and jump fully into the change? Or does the idea of change bring on anxiety and discomfort that you need to entrust to the Lord? Write a letter to the Lord, sharing with him your concerns over the direction you are current-ly going.

2. Both Mother Dolores's and Mama Antula's childhoods greatly shaped their later vocations. How have your early formative experiences affected your own vocation or how you pursue God's calling on your life? Do you have any gifts you are unsure the Lord wants you to share with the world? Ask him about it.

3. How do you reconcile change with what you've identified as your purpose in life? How does prayer factor into this?

CHAPTER 8

Compassionate Caregivers

Friends of the Aging, Declining, and Infirm

"You need to make yourself very little before God."
–St. Jeanne Jugan[1]

There is a beautiful blessing in the benefits of access to better medical care and an improved approach to a healthier lifestyle. Not only are we living longer and enjoying active lifestyles longer, but so are our parents.

This opportunity to enjoy our loved ones longer is not without its challenges. Many of us are encountering generational transitions that are happening closer together. Having raised and launched our children, we barely have time to enjoy the empty nest or retirement before our parents' needs come to the foreground. Although we are living longer, that doesn't necessarily mean we are *living*, in the sense that we have a vibrant connection to our family, friends, and community.

Many of us are facing these challenges with no playbook. There is no generational model for us to follow, so we find ourselves suffering alone and trying our best to move from one challenge to the next. At the same time, our parents are living longer, and in many cases with chronic or severe health challenges. Our generation, having followed opportunities for jobs and relocation, have no experience with the benefits of living within a multigenerational extended family. So when the time comes when our parents are no longer able to safely "age in place," the alternatives can be soul-crushing.

Beginning the Season of Caregiving

The Church teaches the dignity of life in all its experience, from the very youngest and most vulnerable to the very oldest and most vulnerable. This leaves a wide spectrum of humanity in need of our care. We might find ourselves dealing with caregiving for our parents who live far away while simultaneously wanting to be present for our children who are starting their families. If I could solve that problem of bilocation, I would be a billionaire!

What makes these challenges bearable is, of course, the many blessings that come with each season of life. We want to see our children thrive and launch their careers, pursue their dreams, and follow their hearts. We want to see our parents enjoy their later years. And we want to be able to handle this season of our own lives with a grace to be holy examples for our children, and to be obedient to Our Lord's commandment to honor our mother and father. We want to do both with sacrificial and enduring love.

Our closest and most enduring relationship is with our parents. They gave us life and made us the people we are today. We were our most vulnerable with them. We learn to love from them. And when we were past our growing pains and settled into our young adulthood, we once again looked to our parents, learning how to live through their example, and in their final days, learning how to die. That last lesson may be the hardest, but it can also be one of the most beautiful. I am, for practical purposes, as aware of my aging mother's needs as I am of my own. Still, one day, I too will need support and care.

When my father was diagnosed with cancer in his early seventies, the news was devastating for the family. My mother became his caregiver and remained staunchly by his side as he valiantly submitted to treatment after treatment, hoping always for an improvement but faithfully resigned to the Lord's will.

I learned more about how powerful faith can be in the last weeks of my father's life. I learned what it means to surrender, to empty oneself of control and open oneself to the gift of grace. My father, who knew great suffering in his life, also knew from whom his many blessings came. My father came to his death with peace.

My mother, too, taught me enduring lessons during this time of many sacrifices. After fifty-plus years of marriage, they were truly one. My mother accompanied my father on this his final journey, again rarely leaving his side. She attended to his every need. His suffering became her suffering. And her suffering became his. Of course, their mutual sufferings did not cancel each other out— yet there was beauty in them. It was their last dance, if you will, delicate and intimate, and although my siblings and the family watched from afar, and caught the crescendos in the beginning that turned more and more into slow and deliberate steps, it remained a private and beautiful dance with music heard only by them.

What I learned is the power and grace of a sacramental marriage, and the blessing of accompanying each other on the journey home to heaven.

My Second Act seems to be composed of a number of themes, all of them precious opportunities for self-giving. I revel in our grandchildren and support my mother's needs, physically when I can but mostly as a prayer warrior for my sister, who carries the majority of the responsibility for her care. I am also enjoying an exciting time of mentoring writers in my work as editor for CatholicMom.com.

The time spent in these endeavors goes by so quickly I barely notice it. I have fun and come away with a wonderful, warm feeling of contentment and fulfillment, but some days it is exhausting. I think it's important for us to hear this, to acknowledge that the time we spend in caregiving also takes a physical and mental toll.

As I enter a new phase of caregiving for my husband, I am now carrying a larger load of the physical needs of the household while he carries the mental load. Somewhere in between is the delicate dance of providing for his needs, which are gradually increasing as his health declines, while also respecting his dignity. I don't always get it right, but we each ask for forgiveness when it goes awry in one direction or the other, and then, as so many saints have suggested, we begin again.

We begin again often. Caregiving is a grind, and when you are caring for a loved one—in my case, my husband—there are many gray areas. I don't second-guess myself much, but there are times, upon reflection, when I might ask myself, "Am I doing this because he needs me, or am I doing this as an act of service because I love him and want to?" The big question is, Why can't it be both? The bigger question is, Why does it matter?

I think it matters a lot, actually. There have been a few times when I have felt my personal identity disappear into the role of caregiver, and a tiny voice, swallowed up by all the things that need to be done cries out, "But what about me?"

It's in those times that I hold on, sometimes very tightly, to my real identity as a child of God, and let him know I am hurting. We will read next that Rosalynn Carter's Second Act was all about alleviating this pain, and that the featured saint, Jeanne Jugan, made herself little—as little as possible—until it was just her and God.

I want to make myself little, but sometimes I need help.

Rosalynn Carter: A Lifelong Collaboration

I grew up in Atlanta, Georgia, when Jimmy Carter was governor. His picture was in our social studies classroom. Everywhere else, there was a picture of Pope Paul VI.

We moved to Florida right before Carter became president. I didn't care much about politics as a teenager, and other than comments I picked up from adults, couldn't say much about his presidency, but I do recall the First Lady. Mrs. Carter was the consummate southern lady. Her charm was in her demure countenance and her quiet voice. She was just like all the moms of my schoolmates: same demure countenance, same quiet voice.

I knew what that meant. There was a formidable woman behind all that grace.

Eleanor Rosalynn Smith was born on August 18, 1927, in the farming community of Plains, Georgia. Her father was a farmer and mechanic, and her mother was a homemaker. Rosalynn was the oldest of four children. Her father died of leukemia when she was just thirteen years old, and she started working to help her mother make ends meet. By economic standards we would call them poor, but the small-town community kept the family from feeling the desperate effects of poverty.

Rosalynn loved architecture and aspired to attending college to study design, but she met her future husband, Jimmy Carter, a cadet at the Naval Academy, at the end of her first year. They quickly fell in love and were married a year later. She left school to follow him in his military career. The couple had three boys in the early years of their marriage, and then later, they had a daughter. Despite the responsibilities of raising a family with a husband in the military, Rosalynn continued her education with home programs.

When her father-in-law died, the couple returned to Plains to take over the family business, where Rosalynn became the company bookkeeper. Rosalynn demonstrated very early in their marriage that theirs was a collaboration, and she took an active part in this partnership. It would prove to be a lifelong partnership of mutual respect and success with her husband, Jimmy. Decades of partnership prepared them for entering a new era in politics.

As First Lady of Georgia, Mrs. Carter worked hard to bring attention to mental health issues. Through her advocacy, she worked not only to improve access to mental health support, but also to remove the stigma associated with mental illness. She worked to normalize seeking help for depression and to educate the public on mental illness. This project continued through her tenure of First Lady during her husband's presidency, bringing advocacy and education to the national stage. She kept things moving for the family and the business as Jimmy pursued a political career in the Georgia legislature. What was remarkable at the time, and throughout his runs for the governorship and the presidency, is that Rosalynn also actively campaigned for him!

Theirs was truly a partnership, and so it's no surprise that after his presidency, Jimmy would become his wife's greatest supporter as they would work as a team, first on the Carter Center, and then on the Rosalynn Carter Institute for Caregivers.

Rosalynn Carter's Second Act

Rosalynn had a tender heart for both the elderly and their caregivers. She understood firsthand the stress experienced by caregivers. When she was a young girl, she helped her mother nurse her father through his final illness, and in subsequent years took care of other family members with cancer. She also cared for her own mother until she passed away at the age of ninety-four. Perhaps because Rosalynn had firsthand experience with caregiving, she extended compassion to the American people. She observed, "So many people giving care to their loved ones feel isolated, inadequate, despairing. At a time when more and more Americans are called on to give care, it is critically important that we do all we can to support caregivers." She was moved to ease this burden.[2]

In time, the Carter Center became not just the presidential library but a community resource center. Rosalynn was later empowered to build her institute for caregivers. Founded in 1987, the Rosalynn Carter Institute for Caregivers was instrumental decades ago for providing support and resources for caregivers that are widely recognized as necessary today. My own circumstances make this a cause close to my heart. When caregivers receive training, help, and respite, the quality of care for their charges also improves.

Rosalynn Carter's quiet influence in the White House extended far beyond what might have been expected of her as a one-term First Lady. She influenced what that position would look like in subsequent presidencies by not only taking an informal advisory role alongside her husband but also pursuing her advocacy for mental health as the honorary chair of the President's Commission on Mental Health. She went on to receive a number of awards for her humanitarian efforts, including the Presidential Medal of Freedom and induction into the National Women's Hall of Fame.

Rosalynn died at ninety-six. At this writing, Jimmy is approaching his one hundredth birthday after spending a whole year in hospice care. They were together for seventy-eight years, a lovely witness to the beauty of a marriage aging into its golden years.

At the end of his life, St. John Paul II stated in *Evangelium Vitae* that "every person sincerely open to truth and goodness can, by the light of reason and the hidden action of grace, come to recognize in the natural law written in the heart (cf. Rom 2:14–15) the sacred value of human life from its very beginning until its end, and can affirm the right of every human being to have this primary good respected to the highest degree."[3] Rosalynn worked diligently to make sure this dignity was afforded to the elderly and the mentally ill, and to those caregivers serving their needs.

Rosalynn's life, sometimes played out under the scrutiny of the media as merely the wife of a politician, was a life of deep faith in the Lord, a beautiful commitment to her marriage, a loving friendship with her husband, and a very quiet but efficacious commitment to helping society.

St. Jeanne Jugan: Humility in Action

The story of Jeanne Jugan unfolds in the unlikeliest of ways. Whenever I read about the saints, two things usually stand out. First, they accomplished extraordinary things. Some of these accomplishments tend toward the large and dramatic, while other accomplishments, unseen or barely known, speak to a subtle but powerful heroic virtue: humility. Both are extraordinary.

The second thing I've observed about them is that most saints don't want praise or exaltation for their virtue. They take upon themselves John the Baptist's mantle: "He must increase; I must decrease" (Jn 3:30, NABRE). This is the essence of that noble virtue.

St. Jeanne Jugan lived by this scripture her whole life.

Jeanne Jugan was born in Cancale, France, on October 25, 1792. She lived in this fishing village with her father—a fisherman—her mother, and three siblings—a brother and two sisters. Her father perished at sea when she was only four years old, reducing her family to poverty, but they were buoyed by their faith. Young Jeanne knew the need to work at a young age, and her love of God gave her strength.

As a young woman, she knew God had a plan for her life, and she trusted in this, declining an offer of marriage with a prophetic response: "God wants me for himself. He is keeping me for a work which is not yet founded."[4] And thus began Jeanne's lifework of dedicating herself to the other. While Rosalynn Carter saw the power of working with a partner in marriage, Jeanne opted for a total submission to God.

She knew in her heart she would serve others, and left her home to work as a nurse at La Rosais Hospital in nearby Saint Servan. The work was grueling; no doubt she undertook her role as nurse as a ministry, serving more than just the physical needs of her patients. After six years she had to quit from exhaustion.

In need of work, she took on a position as a servant to Mademoiselle Lecoq, a woman some twenty-five years her senior. Although Jeanne was brought on as a maid, it was Lecoq who actually nursed Jeanne back to good health. Together, they would visit the poor and elderly, serving God's mission joyfully.

In 1835, Mlle Lecoq died when Jeanne was in her early forties. Jeanne inherited what little Lecoq left her, but she still had to work for some wealthy families in Saint Servan.

Some years later, Jeanne moved into a flat with two close friends, Francoise Aubert and Virginie Tredaniel. Up to this point, Jeanne's life had been a dress rehearsal for what was to come. For close to fifty years, she worked at what we might disparagingly call menial labor in order to do her real work of serving those in need.

Jeanne's mission reached a defining moment when she and her friends took in an elderly woman who was blind and in poor health. Soon after that, they took in another elderly woman. Then, a young woman, Madeleine Bourges, moved in to be looked after during an illness, and joined the companions after her recovery. This prompted Jeanne to look for larger accommodations. She had already given away her bed to the blind woman. They needed more room. This first generous act of charity had now grown to be a small community of women.

Jeanne was advised by the Brothers Hospitallers of St. John of God to start a collection for the poor, as more and more requests to be admitted to their care kept coming. That year, 1842, proved to be significant in many ways. The combination of collecting donations and the increase in requests to be admitted to the care of these women led Jeanne and her companions to acquire a former convent, and, with local parish priest, Fr. Auguste Le Paileur, serving as witness, the women drew up a rule and named themselves Servants of the Poor. By the end of the year, they added a new companion to their group, Marie Jamet. Jeanne was also elected as superior of this group.

Meanwhile, their model of care for the elderly not only attracted the poor who had no one to care for them in their old age, but also more women who were drawn to this beautiful service. More houses were opened in surrounding towns. The stage was set for Jeanne's Second Act, as she moved from nurse and maid to founder of a religious order.

Jeanne Jugan's Second Act: The Curtain Rises and Falls

Jeanne and her companions in the Servants of the Poor continued to do good work as news of their efficacy and service grow. And yet, inexplicably, Fr. Le Paileur, acting with no authority other than being the local parish priest, annulled Jeanne's election as superior and appointed the young Marie Jamet to the position. He also arbitrarily changed the name of the group to Sisters of the Poor.

Astonishing, isn't it?

But wait, it gets worse. The very next year, in 1845, Jeanne was awarded the Montyon Prize by the Academie Francaise for her work with the poor and elderly. Thanks in part to the publication of this news, she was able to continue to expand. Jeanne opened more houses to serve the poor and elderly—even as she was being silenced and marginalized by the priest entrusted with the spiritual care of her sisters.

Charles Dickens once famously stated that he wanted to bring Sr. Jeanne to England to demonstrate how to serve the poor, and yet Jeanne was being disparaged by her own, not even included in the first general chapter meeting of the Sisters of the Poor!

Over and over, Jeanne was given the grace of humility as Fr. Le Paileur removed her from her duties and sent her into the towns to collect alms for the houses. One day Jeanne knocked on a wealthy man's door and asked for a donation. His response was a slap! Unperturbed, Jeanne said, "Thank you! That slap was for me. Now give me something for my poor."

There's no doubt Jeanne suffered humiliations, but I like to think there was also a bit of single-mindedness in her mission to serve the poor and elderly. As a young woman she knew God wanted her to found something; now she was living that call. Despite being banished, she continued to exert her influence discretely as an instrument of the Lord. She lived by the credo "Refuse God nothing. We must do all through love."[5] With each success that followed for Jeanne, she saw an even greater prize: an increased accessibility of services for those most in need.

In 1843, the Servants of the Poor were founded with just three women. The following year, the first house was established. By 1850 houses had been established throughout France, and the congregation numbered one hundred sisters.

Why was Fr. Le Paileur so opposed to her? What was motivating him?

Behind the Curtain, the Second Act Continued

In 1851, Jeanne was removed from all activities and commanded to have no further contact with benefactors. She was in her early sixties and at the height of her influence with benefactors when Fr. Le Paileur summoned her and stripped her of everything. She was not to have contact with the benefactors, nor was she to continue in any of her work. She was banished to live among the postulants and novices.

For thirty years, Fr. Le Paileur propagated a false narrative that installed himself as founder and placed Jeanne as merely one of the three women present at the founding. Jeanne accepted this humiliation, but not before making it clear to Fr. Le Paileur that she was fully aware of what was happening. "You have stolen my work from me . . . but I willingly give it to you!" The broader tragedy in this is how the young Marie Jamet was manipulated and participated in the fabrication for almost forty years.

I felt this injustice deeply . . . yet justice prevailed in the end. Fr. Le Paileur become more and more authoritarian, and his behavior drew the attention of persons with influence. An investigation was opened, and the disgraced priest was removed and summoned to Rome, where he was moved to a monastery. Marie Jamet unburdened herself, stating she had been torn between obedience and truth. In her wisdom, Jeanne Jugan stated, "People talk to you about me, but let the matter drop. God knows all." Her peace was in becoming poor, as the poor she served.

Within ten years of its founding, the Sisters of the Poor numbered five hundred and were established internationally. In making herself little, Jeanne exerted a beautiful influence in the formation of the postulants. She took the name Sr. Mary of the Cross, and she bore her cross with grace. Her Second Act was most powerful in its littleness. The strong foundation she laid in those early years carried forth the charism of the Little Sisters. In her exile, she continued the good work, through prayer and formation. One of the novices during this period recalled, "She lived in the presence of God, and was always talking to us about Him."

During all those years Jeanne made herself little, the Little Sisters of the Poor (who added "Little" to their name as an affectionate nod to their humility) made themselves small for the sake of others, continued to grow in France, and expanded internationally. Today, the Little Sisters of the Poor operate in thirty-one countries, with more than 180 homes administered by 2,200 sisters.

I had the pleasure of living in a community served by them, and witnessed their mission statement in action: their yes to life and respect for the dignity of the elderly creates a safe and holy space for those in their care.

Living a life of heroic virtue doesn't always look larger than life. The women in this chapter had an understated, often private expression of their faith, and their influence was extraordinary. God made us for our mission, and he uses us, our talents, our personalities, or uniqueness, for his glory.

QUESTIONS TO PONDER

1. Are you or have you been a caregiver to a loved one or family member? Or perhaps accompanied a loved one who is caregiving? What have your experiences taught you about humility, compassion, and sacrifice?

2. What fears do you have in this role, whether you have already experienced caregiving or believe that you will be providing care for someone close to you? Do you have thoughts about what kind of support you will need? Physical? Financial? Spiritual?[6]

3. How does your faith inform you on this journey? Do you have any devotions, scripture, or saint stories that give you consolation or inspiration?

CHAPTER 9

Spiritual Visionaries

Second Act Spirituality Breathes New Life into Old Traditions

"I remembered looking at the moon and the stars and the beautiful things in nature and saying to myself 'who is the master of all these beautiful things?' And I experienced a great desire to see him and know him and honor him. And now I do know him. Thank you, thank you, my God."

–St. Josephine Bakhita[1]

God's grace and generosity overwhelm me. One of my favorite examples is found in the parable of the laborers in the vineyard (Mt 20:1–16), where Jesus likens the kingdom of heaven to a vineyard. The owner hires workers for the day and offers a good rate. As the day wears on, he hires additional workers, and finally, just as the day is ending, another group of workers join. The owner instructs the foreman to pay the day's wages to all the workers, starting with the last group to join. Regardless of how long they worked, everyone receives the same payment.

This, of course, outrages those who had been in the fields all day. The owner is unmoved, as everyone accepted the fair rate that was offered. He responded that he could be as generous as he wanted to be with his money.

I'm sure as a child I heard this parable many times, but undoubtedly, when I first understood the dynamics at play, I was a teenager firmly ensconced in my "that's not fair" era. My worldly sense of justice overrode the point Jesus made to his disciples—that is, God's grace is a gift that is freely given, not earned. But there is so much more to this parable, layers that are rich with meaning. Each subsequent reading reassures me of God's immeasurable love and mercy for me, *for all of us.*

As I describe in my book *Our Lady of Charity,*[2] I was raised in a loving and faithful Catholic home, where a devotion to Our Lady of Charity was as natural as the air we breathed. In our living room, a painting of the Sacred Heart of Jesus was displayed alongside a copy of a Picasso painted by an artist-friend. We attended Mass on Sundays and holy days, and I attended Catholic schools. Despite this foundation, to my deep regret, I fell away from the faith in my twenties.

In the decade or so I turned away from the sacraments and quit attending Mass, my parents never judged me or nagged me to join them. I'm sure that every Mass they attended with an empty spot in the pew next to them was offered up for me. Every silent prayer at the end of the Prayers of the Faithful included a prayer for me. I can say with absolute certainty that my parents prayed me back into the faith, and for that, I am eternally grateful. Their perseverance, patience, and unwavering faith in God's mercy is the greatest thing they've ever done for me.

You might wonder why the parable of the prodigal son doesn't have the same effect on me. It does, of course. When I returned to the Church, at my first Confession before returning to Mass and receiving the Eucharist, my confessor mentioned the parable in his joy at my return. Not too long after that, I read Henri Nouwen's book *The Return of the Prodigal Son: A Story of Homecoming*, and it gave me great insight, not only in regard to my return but what it meant to the father in the story (my parents), and of course, what it means to my heavenly Father. To be honest, it is in understanding this parable that I am so moved by the parable of the workers.

My sense of justice as a teenager was rooted in my understanding of human justice. Crimes are punished. Good deeds are rewarded. We are paid for our work in proportion to the time and effort we put into it. The Equal Rights Amendment was constantly in the news at that time, and equal pay for equal work was practically a daily mantra in my world. That I should respond to this parable in accordance with the social values at the time makes sense to me—the human condition hasn't changed much in the two thousand years between those workers in the vineyard and the rebellious teenager in the 1970s. It took spiritual maturity for me to see that divine justice, God's justice, is not a quid pro quo response; rather, it is rooted in his generosity and mercy, where we receive not according to our merit, but according to his goodness.

The parable of the workers in the vineyard offers powerful commentary on the inclusive nature of our salvation. The first-hour workers were given the privilege of being hired first. By worldly justice, they could reasonably assume they would also earn the most. Instead, all the workers received divine justice, which valued all persons equally. This was a staggering concept that doubled down when the new workers were paid first! Keeping in mind that the parable is representative of heaven, what we learn here is that those who are used to having the least, whether in opportunities or wealth, will gain in heaven in equal proportion.

What that means to me in matters of faith is overwhelming consolation and joy. Like the prodigal son, I had disparaged what I was given. Like the workers coming in at the last hour, I had missed almost a whole day's labor, and I still got paid. My return to the faith happened overnight, in the sense that I acted quickly on my decision—really, I acted quickly on the prompting of the Holy Spirit for me to go to Confession.

I was at a revival hosted by the Missionary Baptist Church, where my children attended day care. My children had begged us to come to the second night of the event, when they would be singing "This Little Light of Mine." I understood right away that this little performance was an evangelization ploy, but I went anyway, camera at the ready, to take pictures. I figured I'd go and get a few shots of the children singing, then we'd get an ice cream and go home and forget about the whole thing.

As you can imagine, it did not play out like that. Well. We *did* get an ice cream, but first, like St. Paul's legendary fall off his horse, I had my own encounter with the Holy Spirit. The revival, did, in fact, revive my dormant faith. I was convicted by a passionate and charismatic pastor who spoke about God's mercy and love for me, and his yearning to have me respond to his love. The invitation was personalized for me. God spoke to *me*. The miracle, of course, is that God speaks to each of us, by name. He knows us intimately, and his mercy is infinite. Whatever had been keeping me from the Lord was shed in that moment, and I found my way back home.

Naturally, there's more to the story. As I thanked that pastor for his powerful words, I knew that I would be in the confessional the next day. My response to the prompting of the Holy Spirit may have been immediate, but my journey home has been a long process of learning, relearning, perseverance, and above all, grace. It is, in fact, not a done deal, but an ongoing conversion steeped in hope and mercy. I couldn't enter into a Second Act, a second opportunity at living my faith fully, without it.

The inspiring women in this chapter played a significant role in promoting spirituality and Divine Mercy. Both happen to be canonized saints. St. Faustina's devotion to Divine Mercy pairs well with St. Josephine Bakhita's forgiveness and joy in the Lord. While St. Faustina died very young, long before the possibility of a Second Act, her efforts in conveying the truth of Divine Mercy make her a most excellent companion in midlife and beyond, when we are drawn to an internal reckoning of our lives. Her Second Act is a posthumous one, as her vision caught on throughout the world. In contrast, St. Josephine lived a long life, dying at seventy-eight after having survived abduction, enslavement, and unimaginable cruelty before entering the convent in her mid-fifties. In a world desperately in need of mercy, Josephine shows us how to forgive.

St. Faustina: Missionary of Mercy

St. Faustina Kowalska, canonized in 2000, was my conversion companion. Although her cause for canonization was opened in 1968 when I was a little girl, her beatification in 1993 ended up being a part of my reversion to the faith. Just as I experienced a sudden realization that I had been wasting my time away from the faith, twenty-five-year-old Faustina had a moment of reckoning. In a vision from the Lord, Faustina (then Helena) heard Jesus say to her, "How long shall I put up with you and how long will you keep putting me off?"[3] She immediately responded with prayer, and within the year joined the Congregation of the Sisters of Our Lady of Mercy. The rest of her life would be an example of God's transformative power and his boundless mercy.

St. Faustina was born Helena Kowalska on August 25, 1905, in Glogowiec, Poland. She was one of ten children of poor peasants. Despite their poverty, she was encouraged in her faith, exhibiting a deep prayer life from a young age. In fact, she knew she was called to religious life when she was a little girl, although she did not understand what that meant until much later.

At sixteen, Helena finished her schooling and left home to pursue work in nearby villages. She became a housekeeper to several families, both as a means to her own independence and also to help her parents. She had wanted to enter the convent, but her parents did not give her permission. So Helena set aside her dream for a time. While at a dance when she was nineteen, she had that vision of the suffering Christ asking her how long she would continue to put him off, and she realized that it was time to respond. Although she was rejected by several convents, she eventually entered the Congregation of the Sisters of Mercy on August 1, 1925.

Sr. Faustina's role in the convent consisted of menial tasks such as cleaning, cooking, and gardening. Although the convent was filled with all manner of physical trials, she persevered in her commitment to Christ. She remained steadfast in her spiritual formation, developing an interior life that "hid within herself an extraordinary union with God."[4] During this time, Sr. Faustina experienced many mystical encounters with Christ. She kept a journal of these encounters, giving detailed accounts of the visions as well as conversation she had with Jesus. These records of her encounters were later published as *The Diary of Saint Maria Faustina Kowalska: Divine Mercy in My Soul.*

The Divine Mercy Revelations: Entrust Your Second Act

The central focus of these conversations, as recorded in Faustina's diaries, was God's infinite mercy and his desire for all people to *trust* in his mercy. As the Lord continued to expound on the nature of his mercy, Sr. Faustina developed a deeper love for and understanding of what this Divine Mercy meant. It did not come without trials, as she was often met with skepticism from her sisters and her own spiritual directors. Still, she remained steadfast in her commitment to the Lord. Despite being largely misunderstood, Sr. Faustina recorded every encounter with Christ in her diary. Her obedience to his will is exemplified in the prayer to the Divine Mercy: "Jesus, I trust in You."

One of the most powerful entries in her diary details God's plan for Sr. Faustina: "I sent prophets wielding thunderbolts to My people. Today I am sending you with My mercy to the people of the whole world. I do not want to punish aching mankind, but I desire to heal it, pressing it to My Merciful Heart."[5]

This commissioning must have been difficult for Sr. Faustina. She suffered from tuberculosis, a painful and debilitating illness that often left her hospitalized. Despite this, she continued to press forward, recording the Divine Mercy message and offering her own suffering for the salvation of souls. She was committed to offering hope in the unconditional love and forgiveness of God. She wanted to spread the message of mercy to all those who despair, burdened by sin.

I am particularly moved by the Lord's words to her, "I do not want to punish aching mankind, but I desire to heal it, pressing it to My Merciful Heart." I am undone by this imagery of a loving parent clasping his child to his heart. As a visual learner, I often respond better when I can "see" an image, and this is exactly what Sr. Faustina gave us through Our Lord. In 1931, she had a vision of Jesus clothed in vibrant white, with rays of red and blue bursting forth from his heart. In this vision, Jesus told her to commission a painting of this image, with the inscription "Jesus, I trust in You," for all the world to see his outpouring of mercy for the whole world.

The Lord also instructed Sr. Faustina to share the Chaplet of Divine Mercy, a powerful prayer that invokes God's mercy not just on sinners but on the whole world. I was introduced to this prayer by my father, who prayed it daily in the last decade of his life. I adopted his little, but very big, mission after learning about this prayer. I used to make little chaplets, really nothing more than a decade of a rosary with a crucifix on it, as a devotional to carry in a pocket. I would often give them to my father.

He kept me busy. No sooner had I given him a new one than he would give it away and ask for a replacement. One day I asked him why he kept losing the little chaplets. I thought he was misplacing them on a desk or a counter somewhere; after all, they were small and fit easily in the palm of a hand. He told me he was giving them away and teaching about the power of Divine Mercy.

This message of Divine Mercy, intended for the whole world, remained largely behind convent walls for decades. St. Faustina died in 1938 from complications from tuberculosis, and then-Archbishop Karol Wojtyla opened the cause for her canonization in Krakow in 1965. This became a kind of Second Act, completing her commission by establishing Divine Mercy Sunday as a feast day for the Church.

We are all called to be instruments of his mercy here on earth. For many of us, it begins with not just seeking forgiveness, but forgiving others. Sometimes the act of forgiveness seems insurmountable, but we see in another saint, Josephine Bakhita, that as we are forgiven so we should forgive.

St. Josephine Bakhita: Exemplar of Forgiveness

Sometimes I notice things that have a poetic ring to them. In this case, St. Faustina, the woman entrusted to bring the message of Divine Mercy to the world, was canonized the same year as St. Josephine Bakhita, an amazing model of forgiveness. There's beauty and poetry in the connection. Coincidence? Perhaps God-incidence.

Bakhita was born circa 1869 in Olgossa in the Darfur region of Sudan. Her family was affluent, perhaps a factor leading to her abduction by Arab slave traders, possibly Baggara, when she was a little girl of seven. One of her sisters had also been kidnapped some years before that. In the unimaginable aftermath of being taken from her family, the seven-year-old forgot her name, and her captors, making fun of her and her situation, named her Bakhita, which means "fortunate." Her life would be anything but fortunate over the ensuing decades.

Born years after the 1863 Emancipation Proclamation in the United States, Bakhita's story reminds us of the horrors and ravages of human trafficking that continue throughout the world to this day. She was sold numerous times and suffered all kinds of inhumane treatment and cruelty, including being tortured by one of her captives, who deeply scarred her, tattooing her body with a razor and salt. In response to that mutilation, Bakhita said, "It seemed I was dying at every moment, especially when they rubbed in the salt. . . . I can honestly say that the reason I did not die was that the Lord miraculously destined me for better things."[6]

As I reflect upon about this horrific experience, I am reminded that Our Lord, who told St. Faustina he wanted to heal the sinner with his Divine Mercy, made this healing available even to souls like those who inflicted these horrors on Bakhita.

Remarkably, the accounts of her suffering, when she spoke of it in her later years, are not tinged with anger or resentment. In her autobiography, she shares two encounters with a being whom she believes to be her guardian angel. In one instance, when she and other slaves were running from their captors in the night, she saw a shining figure that seemed to be leading her through the forest. She felt a great peace within and trusted the figure, although she did not share what she had seen. Many years later, while living in the convent, she saw the same figure, which stood beside her and then disappeared.

Bakhita also credits her guardian angel with protecting her from wild animals, and on at least one occasion from sexual assault, an all-too-common experience for female slaves. When the Turk who had ordered the ritual tattooing and scarring saw that she had started developing breasts, he had Bakhita brought to him. On several occasions he brutally manhandled her, then sent her away. She maintained for the rest of her life that she had been spared from rape.

In 1883, when she was about fourteen, Callisto Legnani, an Italian consul, bought the young woman to be his household servant. For Bakhita, it was a reprieve from the physical abuses that had been a part of her life since the abduction. Legnani treated her with kindness, although she remained a slave. A couple of years later, when his tour was over, he returned to Italy and brought Bakhita with him. There, Legnani gifted her to the Michieli family, who delighted in Bakhita and put her to work. It was in the Michieli household where Bakhita first learned about Christianity.

Bahkita lived with the Michielis for about three and half years. She started off as a housemaid, but when their daughter was born, Bakhita became her nanny. It was in those years that Bakhita met the estate manager for the Michielis, Illuminato Checchini. He was probably her first encounter with Christianity, in that he had a heart for the plight of the peasant, and Bakhita, as a slave, was even less than a peasant. Checchini gave Bakhita a crucifix and encouraged her to say her daily prayers with her little charge. In fact, Checchini's role in Bakhita's life was more as a father figure. He sponsored her throughout her catechumenate and supported her entry into the convent. In short, he became her family, and a rich correspondence with his children and grandchildren reveal a loving familial relationship among them.

At about this time, the Michielis were preparing to move back to Africa. As the parents traveled back and forth between the two continents, Bakhita was left to care for the child until the household was ready to move permanently to her homeland. Bakhita and her charge were installed in the boardinghouse of the school run by the Canossian Daughters of Charity. It was there that Bakhita truly felt at home, and she presented herself for baptism. And thus, Bakhita entered the catechumenate. When the Michielis returned and discovered that Bakhita was on her way to becoming a Christian, they demanded her return. However, slavery was illegal in Venice, and the sisters took the family to court. In a landmark ruling, Bakhita's freedom was secured.

A Second Act of Faith

Bakhita was baptized in 1890, taking the name Josephine for St. Joseph, and in 1896 she joined the Canossian Daughters of Charity. For the next fifty years, Sr. Josephine worked tirelessly to ease the burden for the poor and needy in their care. In the course of those many years, Sr. Josephine traveled extensively, telling her story. When asked what she would say to her captors were she to encounter them, her response captured the essence of forgiveness: "If I were to meet those who kidnapped me, and even those who tortured me, I would kneel and kiss their hands. For, if these things had not happened, I would not have been a Christian and a religious today."[7] Sr. Josephine rose above her suffering and responded to her captives with love. Her witness is a profound message of forgiveness.

QUESTIONS TO PONDER

1. Contemplate the Divine Mercy image, the image that Jesus instructed St. Faustina to have commissioned to spread the message of his Divine Mercy. Has this message influenced the way you approach forgiveness?

2. St. Josephine spent the rest of her life among her religious sisters in Italy, and never saw her homeland again. Yet for the rest of her life, she expressed gratitude toward those who had enslaved her, for it led her to Jesus. What does this say to you?

3. How does forgiving—and being forgiven—free you?

CHAPTER 10

Inspired Mentors

Because It's Never Too Late to Be a Badass

"Let yourself be loved."

–St. Elizabeth of the Trinity[1]

Basketball has always been a part of my life. Some of my earliest childhood memories involve foul shots and layups. There's a picture of me as a toddler, barely able to walk, with a ball at my side. There's a baby doll next to me, too, but as far as childhood games and pastimes go, basketball was clearly my first love.

The truth is, my memories of basketball are inexorably intertwined with the sisters who taught me, and the coaches who saw in me a talent beyond dribbling and shooting. There are many reasons to recommend a parochial school education, but I will always be especially grateful for the impact that playing basketball had on my formation. When the academics proved difficult, and the mysteries of the faith eluded my grasp, I had the constancy of basketball to keep me motivated.

I was really pretty good. The kind of good that could have gone to my head. Thankfully, basketball is a team sport with lots of opportunities for substitutions and sitting out a quarter to keep a young ego in check. I learned a lot on the court and on the bench. Naturally, I loved to win, but playing is what brought me joy.

By the time I was in what we would now call middle school, social dynamics changed along with changing bodies. Tall and slender, I found myself the target of a clever bully who knew how to hurt with words. Thankfully, the bullying ended the following year as abruptly as it started, but the damage to my self-esteem lasted a long time. Only in more recent years could I look back on that time with a bit of objectivity and understand that the bully must have been struggling as much as I was.

I owe a great debt to my coaches and teachers, who may not have known the details of what had been going on but tapped into the game I loved to help me navigate a tough period in my development. Being team captain not only honed my leadership skills but also taught me the importance of empathy, two skills I carried off the court.

Forming Disciples in Community

The basketball fever at my elementary school was fueled by the last game of the season, a family night event we all looked forward to, which started with a friendly game between fathers and sons. One or two of the young priests would join in the fun, and we were all astonished to see them in shorts and t-shirts, and not their usual clerics. If that was a shock for us, imagine our sheer delight when the big event started: the faculty versus the eighth-grade girls.

That game was better than a championship tournament. When those sisters came out on the court in their long shorts and short veils, we were absolutely stricken. As I look back on it, I realize these women were much, much younger than I thought. Most of them were in their late twenties and early thirties, and I am sure they enjoyed themselves immensely. I can't for the life of me remember who won the game. It doesn't matter; we were enjoying each other, having fun and fellowship. It is in the beauty of that community coming together to rejoice that I learned an important lesson that has taken an entire lifetime to come to maturity: ours is a joyful faith. It is not without its trials or its difficulties in understanding and applying the foundational tenets too often misunderstood by the faithful themselves, let alone society, but it is a faith that is filled with hope and love. A faith that forms disciples. This lesson would inform my approach to education, whether in the classroom or on the court, and also influenced me later in life when I transitioned away from education and into women's ministry.

The Grace of Second Chances and Final Acts

I have a soft spot for the religious sisters who educated me, the Grey Nuns of the Sacred Heart. Some of them were old-school stern, but I say with great confidence that these women were filled with the joy of the Lord. That spilled out into the energy on the court in that famous faculty game, but it was also in the classroom, and in the community where their witness was a loving gesture of support and faith.

This is the lesson that was ingrained in me—that our God is a loving God, a God of second chances, a God who is merciful.

When I look back on my life and see the times I have reset and entered a season of new opportunities and new beginnings, I bring with me all the old lessons, too. Perhaps we attribute wisdom to our elders as some kind of final gift (it is, after all, a gift of the Holy Spirit), when it is a way of looking at life with the benefit of experience.

I think the most beautiful part of growing old is growing in confidence and embracing a level of boldness that carries us into this, perhaps *our final act*. Sometimes I hear from my peers— women with good health and still quite a bit of verve and drive—"I don't care," as a kind of dismissive rallying cry, an expression of the desire to do what we want. The thing is, I do care, and they do, too. Perhaps it is a matter of reframing.

I understand it. While I still consider myself too young to think of a "final act," I cannot ignore the fact that the timeline has shifted and I now have many more years behind me than ahead of me. Or maybe not. A dear friend of mine reminds me that I'm not writing that script. I don't have to try too hard to see evidence of this when I see the lifetime of service from the women included in this book.

That's why I look to role models and saints who approach life with joy, who grab it with a boisterous energy and laugh and enjoy the present, and all the moments throughout the day that make them feel alive. I want saints who delight in the love of our Father, and thus become conduits of that love around them.

Sr. Jean Dolores Schmidt: A Nun for All Seasons

What fan of college basketball is not familiar with Sr. Jean Dolores Schmidt, the chaplain for the Loyola University Chicago Ramblers?

She's become a kind of mascot, with her own bobblehead and fans that carry the BigHead posters of her face to basketball games. Sr. Jean is certainly deserving of this love from the Loyola students and fans of the Ramblers basketball team. At the beautiful age of 104, she'd be the first to tell you that working with young people has kept her young in spirit.

While I'm trying to figure out what my next act might be, Sr. Jean is relishing what might be her third or fourth act! Honestly, her energy and commitment embody everything I'd love to be in this new season of my life.

Sr. Jean came onto the national sports scene at the NCAA basketball tournament in 2018, charming fans who were both delighted and curious about this elderly religious sister with a knowledge of basketball who was not only cheering on her team but was there as chaplain and scout. At the tournament in 2021, as chaplain, she gave an iconic pregame prayer that integrated a scouting report on the opponents, the Illini. You don't have to know much about basketball to realize this was both empowering to the Ramblers and probably a little demoralizing to their opponents. For the record, the Ramblers defeated the Illini in that game.

No kidding, how does a nun happen to know so much about the game? She played basketball in high school in the 1930s! That explains it. I immediately felt an affinity for her, and learned that we also share a background in education.

After she graduated high school in 1937, Sr. Jean entered the Sisters of Charity of the Blessed Virgin Mary convent in Iowa and became a teacher. She taught elementary school in California, where she also coached women's basketball and other sports, and to my amusement, coached yo-yo. There's a certain seriousness in training for sports such as basketball, softball, or soccer. Strategies, practice schedules, and running plays require commitment and study. That somehow the yo-yo is included in her resume speaks to a whimsical side to her that is disarming.

In 1961, Sr. Jean joined the faculty of Mundelein College in Chicago. This transition to teaching college must have been a challenging one. I know firsthand that the most jarring transition to higher education is the sheer size of the institution and how easily a student might feel lost in the crowd. The relational nature of teaching children doesn't always translate to the adult learner. Yet, young adults also need encouragement. Sr. Jean's advice to them resonates with me: "That's being a person for others by just being yourself. . . . That's the way I am. I have to be myself. I tell students that—you'll see people that you admire, you can do some of the things they do, but you have to be yourself. God made you the person who you are."[2]

Within a decade, Sr. Jean had yet another professional transition, as she moved into higher education administration. It is no small accomplishment to become a dean at a college, but she continued on that track, finally becoming vice president of Academic Affairs. When Mundelein merged with Loyola University Chicago in 1991, she came on board as assistant dean and worked as an academic advisor.

A Second Act Booster Shooter

You might think that's quite a step down, but considering Sr. Jean's advice to be the person God made you to be, well, that was perhaps exactly who the students needed *her* to be. Advisement is rarely more than a brief conversation with some guidance about coursework. I can't imagine that was the experience she gave her students.

By now Sr. Jean was in her seventies and ready to wind down her busy schedule. In fact, as her seventy-fifth birthday approached and she was, indeed, going to retire, she embraced a new role as tutor to help players retain academic eligibility on the men's and women's basketball teams. What a magnificent way to bring a lifetime's work together, using all her knowledge in one place to help these young people. She referred to herself as the "Booster Shooter."

Her story doesn't end there. Sr. Jean went on to become the chaplain for the men's team, and began an initiative called SMILE (Students Moving into the Lives of the Elderly), a wonderful program pairing students from the university with residents of the local retirement home.

Fast-forward to that NCAA championship tournament where the world became enthralled with her, and to the present. At 104 years old, she is still teaching and guiding others through her memoir, *Wake Up With Purpose! What I've Learned in My First Hundred Years.*

Sr. Jean has enjoyed an extraordinarily long life, and no doubt been a source of inspiration and encouragement for scores of students. When I look at her accomplishments, I don't wish to be a hundred as a personal goal. Instead, I aspire to live the years ahead of with me the same joy for serving others as Sr. Jean demonstrates. She shared God's love for us with her students, celebrating our lovableness in God's eyes. I know, because I've had many Sr. Jeans in my life.

St. Elizabeth of the Trinity: Age is Relative

You might say that age is relative when looking at Sr. Jean's long life and how she was accomplishing extraordinary things at twenty-six, or seventy-five, or 103. But what happens when our life on earth is short? The same axiom applies.

St. Elizabeth of the Trinity, a Discalced Carmelite nun, was born in July of 1880. Her father was a military official who died when Elizabeth was a child. Her mother, a widow with two young girls, moved her little family to Dijon, France, where Elizabeth bloomed. There was a Carmelite monastery next to their home, and she longed to join it. She was drawn to the Carmelite charism of contemplation, community, and service. Convicted, Elizabeth declared that one day she would join this monastery.

Although Elizabeth had many suitors, she insisted on entering Carmel. Not only did she announce that she wanted to be a religious at the tender age of seven, at thirteen she gave herself completely to Jesus with a vow of virginity. She was ready to enter the monastery next door, but her mother insisted that she wait. Meanwhile, Elizabeth's life as a young woman was filled with the usual responsibilities in a household, but she also excelled at the piano and was a gifted musician. She sang in the church choir and taught catechism to the local children.

The nuns at the monastery recognized her prayerfulness, and they shared with her a treatise of sorts written by one of the nuns at another monastery that they had been sharing among themselves. It was St. Thérèse of Lisieux's *Story of a Soul*. Imagine that—they were contemporaries! Elizabeth had a deep spirituality and a devotion to the Holy Trinity that continued to grow during those years as she led her life as daughter and sister and, no doubt, friend, anticipating the day she would enter the convent.

"We must be mindful of how God is in us in the most intimate way and go about everything with him," Elizabeth wrote. "Then life is never banal. Even in ordinary tasks, because you do not live for these things, you will go beyond them."[3]

Elizabeth had her heart set on one thing: the Trinity. Having obtained her mother's consent, she entered Carmel when she turned twenty-one years old. Almost immediately, she fell ill from a mysterious stomach ailment. She likely suffered from Addison's disease, an illness that stems from a lack of a hormone that regulates cortisol. Today, a hormone treatment would be prescribed, but this unchecked illness ravaged Elizabeth's body and she succumbed to it within five years.

Joyful Suffering for Love of God

In the midst of this illness, Elizabeth sought to grow deeper in love with the Trinity. From an early age, Elizabeth had a contemplative spirit that yearned for closeness with God. She had a preternatural understanding of God's indwelling in her soul, and remarked, "I have found my heaven on earth, since heaven is God, and God is in my soul." Living, as she did, with this understanding of God within her, Elizabeth radiated joy.

Think for a moment of all the truly joyful saints. Many of them died quite young, such as St. Elizabeth. Meanwhile, I feel it has taken my whole life to just begin to understand that this joy, as St. Elizabeth points out, is to be expressed in all things: "Every happening, every event, every suffering as also every joy, is a sacrament that gives God to the soul." I can't help but think that this joy stems from gratitude for God's unconditional, abundant love.

I'm drawn to St. Elizabeth because of her spirituality. There's simplicity in her basic message that God is already within us. Everything else comes from that; we are a resting place for our Triune God: he rests in us, and we in him. I can see these words on the page and hear them spoken and yet I hold out, not quite feeling worthy of this love. And that is where St. Elizabeth grabbed me and shook me, affectionately and not too hard, to hear what I've been told my whole life: You are loved. You are God's beloved. Cue Elizabeth's assertive voice: "Let yourself be loved."

Those simple words, spoken with love, disarm me. There are so many ways in which I put up a wall to this love. Sin, in all its forms, builds that wall, brick by brick. My concupiscence is the mortar that sets it. And yet, St. Elizabeth tells me that God is already residing in my soul. No wall can shut him out. I am undone.

Heaven's Second Act: Let Yourself Be Loved

St. Elizabeth used this entreaty, "Let yourself be loved," often in her writings. In a letter to her prioress, Mother Germaine, who was suffering from anxiety, Elizabeth wrote encouragingly, "If you faithfully believe that He is still working, that He is loving you just the same, and even more: because His love is free and that is how He wants to be magnified in you; and you will *let yourself be loved.*"[4] She repeated that last line numerous times, as if to drive home a point the prioress was resisting. Aren't we all one with that prioress, resisting what is right in front of us: the God who made us in his image, to love and be loved. What strikes me about St. Elizabeth's letter is a tender care for her prioress, a letter written with such intimacy as one might see between friends.

I find this advice from St. Elizabeth especially meaningful for us as we age. Ideally, we will age gracefully, surrounded by loved ones. That is certainly my hope. However, the harsh reality for many is an old age filled with isolation and loneliness. It is in these circumstances that I find St. Elizabeth's encouragement heartwarming and charitable. We are not alone. Our God who loves us, who wants to love us, is present within us.

Elizabeth died at the age young age of twenty-six, barely into her first act. Sr. Jean lived past the age of one hundred, accomplishing many things in her lifetime. Both women are sources of inspiration for me. Sr. Jean, because she demonstrates that a long life is a source of opportunity to serve the Lord; and St. Elizabeth, because she crammed a lifetime into a short period of time. I believe that St. Elizabeth's death put her straight into *her* Second Act: praying for us in heaven.

As Dr. Anthony Lilles, a seminary professor and expert in Elizabeth's spirituality, has put it, "The Lord has chosen to answer her prayers for us . . . before she died, when she was suffering with Addison's disease, she wrote that it would increase her joy in heaven if people asked for her help."[5] What better companion for our lives than a friend praying for us in heaven?

These holy women inspire me and have taught me that where there is joy, there is love, and where there is love, there is God.

> Let us live with God as with a friend, let us make our faith a living faith in order to be in communion with Him through everything, for that is what makes us saints. We possess our Heaven within us. . . . The day I understood that everything became clear to me. I would like to whisper this secret to those I love so they too might always cling to God through everything. (St. Elizabeth of the Trinity, Letter 122)

QUESTIONS TO PONDER

1. Perhaps the best way to grow old is with God as a companion and friend. St. Elizabeth tells us that we already have that Friend residing in our soul. How does God want you to let yourself be loved by him today?

2. Reflect upon your beliefs and attitudes about aging. Are you looking forward to retiring or an opportunity to do something new? Is it possibly a little bit of both?

3. What aspirations or goals have you set for your later years? How does this include God? How would you describe your spirituality?

Conclusion

Tempus Fugit; Memento Mori

My Second Act began with a stroke of grace—a miracle health scare that served as a catalyst for change in my physical health, mental well-being, and spiritual growth. I wasn't expecting a fun (yet challenging) journey. Entering middle age and beyond seemed far away for me. In my mind, I'm in my thirties, enjoying life without a care. My knees scream otherwise, and so I've had to adjust to a few sobering moments that have reminded me that *tempus fugit* is more than a pithy Latin phrase.

As a Catholic, I follow the phrase *tempus fugit* with another: *memento mori.* I'm comfortable with the passage of time, but the second half, "remember death," is perhaps more sobering than I wish. As so many things in our faith that might look a little daunting, the truth is the truth, and we are, inevitably, going to die someday. I'm just not in a hurry.

Nevertheless, this reminder of the swift passage of time and the inevitability of death encourages me to live a life of virtue. I often turn to the saints for companionship, but more than that, I seek saints who have experienced some of the same or similar circumstance as me. It was natural for me to seek saints who would be companions for me in this next stage of my life. Among them, I hoped to find models of the virtues I would need for my Second Act. I looked for sympathetic prayer partners who would pray for me. Women with whom I shared similarities or an affinity for the same things. Women saints who had a little bit more experience, a little bit more wisdom, and a little bit more mileage.

Saints whose humanity with all its beautiful mess reminds me that I, too, have the stuff of sainthood inside me, if I would let it out and surrender myself to God's will, open myself to his abundant mercy and lavish grace.

Silly me, I thought an academic search would lead me to these saints. True, one or two popped up, saints I was familiar with, but then something amazing happened. Suddenly, the saints started coming to *me*. They would repeatedly show up in my social media feeds. Friends would send me quotes attributed to them. One friend kept recommending a book about a saint's life. Cookies at a bookstore checkout claimed to be a saint's recipe.

Finally, I could not escape literature about a saint for whom I had little regard. Those are the dangerous ones. Those are the saints who really want to get your attention. They really want to be friends with me, and the saints want to be friends with you, too.

Just as I foster friendships with persons who have the same interests as me, I look to the saints for the same kind of attraction. I pull away the veil of mystery that we so often attribute to saints, and look for their humanity. It is a shared humanity, and since they got it right and lived lives of heroic virtue, I want to learn as much as I can from them.

- Like **St. Hildegard of Bingen**, I want to try everything. I'm learning to be a gardener and taking up crafts such as papermaking and bookbinding. I even bought some fancy pencils to return to my childhood love of sketching.

- **St. Olga** reminds me that change can be good. Thankfully, I don't have a wildly violent past, but in her story I learned that we are not defined by our own sinful deeds, and can grow in holiness with each new year.

- Leaning into our gifts with humility and trust in the Lord was a hallmark of **St. Marianne Cope's** life. She led with perseverance, served with courage, and entered her Second Act in Hawaii with the same unwavering enthusiasm and love that she started with in the classroom.

- **Sr. Thea Bowman** taught me a powerful lesson in communication. As a child, she immersed herself in her community, so that as an adult she could not only advocate for African American inclusion and representation in the Church but also bring the beauty of her cultural traditions into the Eucharistic celebration to be a part of the Catholic experience, not set them apart in isolated or separate experiences.

- Thanks to **Dorothy Day**, I learned an important lesson in the breadth of God's love for us, and how, as his children, there is room for each and every one of us in his heart and in his Church.

- **Mama Antula** charmed me with her youthful rejection of her society's expectations, but the mature woman inspires me as an example of perseverance and conviction. Rather than slowing down, Mama Antula pushed forward in her evangelization efforts.

- Grace defines **Elisabeth Leseur's** life. She suffered physically and spiritually, but it was grace that gave her all she needed in order to endure devastating illness and spiritual isolation. My physical ailments have caused suffering in my life, but my spiritual challenges, periods in my life when I felt adrift in my faith, were alleviated through spiritual journaling. Like Elisabeth, I found consolation in a secret diary, too. I discovered the best way to sort through my thoughts is on the page in a dialogue with Our Lord.

- **St. Jeanne Jugan** made herself small. Her beautiful care of the sick and elderly especially accompanies me in my personal life with an aging mother experiencing dementia and with my husband who has ALS (amyotrophic lateral sclerosis). Her example of making herself small and emptying herself for the Lord encourages me to do the same for those I love as I endeavor to bring his light into their lives.

- The lesson in forgiveness modeled by **St. Josephine Bakhita** stirs my soul. Anyone would be embittered by the circumstance in her life, and yet she forgave her captors. She attained freedom from slavery, but more than that, she found freedom in Christ.

- **St. Elizabeth of the Trinity's** emphasis on our lovability, and the indwelling of the Trinity within us, reframes my relationship with God. He isn't just with me, he resides deep within my soul.

The amazing women and extraordinary saints in this book have inspired me, encouraged me, taught me about confidence, perseverance, courage, and most of all, faith. Their companionship by example and through prayer have buoyed me and will continue to do so, and I am grateful for the opportunity to share them with you.

I'm in the midst of my Second Act, and at this writing I am inspired to go as far as I can. I'm also looking forward to the possibility of a third and even a fourth act! What I'm certain of is that I am not ready for the words "the end." How about you?

To that end, I offer this little "Litany of the Second Act." Won't you pray with me?

> **Servant of God Elisabeth Leseur,** woman of faith and resilience, pray for me when I am suffering physically and spiritually, that I might have the grace I need to persevere.

> **St. Hildegard of Bingen,** scholar and healer, pray for me as I explore new gifts and interests in my Second Act, that my mind would stay strong and supple.

> **St. Olga of Kyiv,** fearless warrior and earnest convert, pray for me that I might fight my earthly battles with heavenly zeal, with a heart soft and open to the Lord.

> **St. Marianne Cope,** motherly of heart, pray for me that I might serve with courage as a true spiritual mother, content to watch all those in my care thrive and grow.

> **Servant of God Thea Bowman,** exuberant singer and joyful teacher, pray for me that I would never draw back from bringing justice and holy joy into my corner of the world.

> **Servant of God Dorothy Day,** pray for me that I might not be defined by my mistakes, but by my earnest efforts to lift up the lowly and helpless.

St. Maria Antonia de Paz y Figueroa, pray for me that I would never be held back by fear of where a path might take me. Help me to trust in the One who leads.

St. Jeanne Jugan, lover of the helpless and diminished, pray for me that I might have the inner resources I need to love and care for those in my life who need my help.

St. Josephine Bakhita, apostle of forgiveness, pray for me that my soul might stir with the mercy of God, that I might find the freedom of forgiveness in every area of my life.

St. Elizabeth of the Trinity, who plumbed the depth and breadth of the mystery of God, pray for me that I might receive and revel in his abundant love for me, and embrace the goodness that is to be found in living every moment in anticipation of heaven.

All these things I pray in the name of the Father, and the Son, and the Holy Spirit. Amen!

All you saints of the Second Act, pray for us!

Acknowledgments

This book would not have come to life without the love and support of so many generous people. My heartfelt gratitude goes first to my husband, children, and extended family, whose encouragement has been a steadfast presence, lifting me when I needed it most. To my dear friend and editor Heidi Hess Saxton—our shared ideas and laughter have been invaluable, inspiring me to dive deeper, guiding me in the finer points of crafting this book. To the wonderful team at Ave Maria Press, who took a working manuscript and turned it into a book I am proud of. To my dear girlfriends who have walked with me through many of the experiences in this book. Finally, to every reader who finds a spark here, know that you, too, are part of this journey.

Notes

1. A Stroke of Grace: Resilient Women Who Persevered

1. Elisabeth Leseur, *The Secret Diary of Elisabeth Leseur: The Woman Whose Goodness Changed Her Husband from Atheist to Priest* (Manchester, NH: Sophia Institute Press, 2002), 271–272.

2. Colleen Cheslak, "Hedy Lamarr," National Women's History Museum, 2018, https://www.womenshistory.org/education-resources/biographies/hedy-lamarr.

3. The Navy ultimately rejected the idea, but Lamarr and Antheil gained a US patent for it, although the patent expired without their making any money on the science.

4. "Hedy Lamarr and Jean Harlow: The Inspiration for Catwoman," CMG Worldwide, December 11, 2023, https://www.cmgworldwide.com/2023/12/11/hedy-lamarr-jean-harlow-the-inspiration-for-catwoman.

5. "Hathaway's Catwoman Inspired by Lamarr," IMDb, December 30, 2011, https://www.imdb.com/news/ni20296435/.

6. Belle Hutton, "The 1940s Hollywood Actress Who Invented Technology for WiFi," *AnOther Magazine*, November 24, 2017, https://www.anothermag.com/fashion-beauty/10389/the-1940s-hollywood-actress-who-invented-technology-for-wifi.

7. Quoted in Bernadette Chovelon, *Salt and Light: The Spiritual Journey of Élisabeth and Félix Leseur* (San Francisco: Ignatius Press, 2020), 138.

2. Pioneering Scientists Who Kept Their Minds Strong

1. Quoted in Becca Perry-Hill, "Hildegard, Our Guide," Lumunos, https://www.lumunos.org/single-post/2019/03/07/hildegard-our-guide.

2. Docter Y, "Marie Curie's Notebooks," American Council of Science and Health, January 3, 2022, https://www.acsh.org/news/2022/01/03/marie-curie%E2%80%99s-notebooks-16033.

3. Susan Quinn, *Marie Curie: A Life* (New York: Simon and Schuster, 1995).

3. Visionary Leaders Who Were Unafraid to Kick Butt and Take Names

1. Quoted in *The Russian Primary Chronicle: Laurentian Text*, trans. and ed. Samuel Hazzard Cross and Olgerd P. Sherbowitz-Wetzor (Cambridge, MA: Medieval Academy of America, 1953), 83.

2. Excerpt from Letter to President McKinley Protesting the Annexation of Hawaii, 1897, as quoted in Kalewa Correa, "Queen Lili'uokalai: Hawaii's Only Reigning Queen," Smithsonian American Women's History Museum, https://womenshistory.si.edu/herstory/activism/object/queen-liliuokalani.

4. Dedicated Mothers Who Embodied "Love in the Trenches"

1. Quoted in Fran Gangloff, *Mission of Grace: The Story of Saint Marianne Cope* (Cincinnati: Franciscan Media, 2023).

5. Extraordinary Artists: Creatives Who Made the World Better

1. Thea Bowman, "Experiencing Black Spirituality: Flying with the Metaphor," selected and arranged by Lynne Holtzman, in *Thea Bowman: Handing on Her Legacy*, ed. Christian Koontz (Kansas City, MO: Sheed and Ward, 1991), 5.

2. "Sr. Thea Bowman's Address to the U.S. Bishop's Conference," June 1989, Subcommittee on African American Affairs, USCCB, https://www.usccb.org/resources/Transcript-Sr-Thea-Bowman-June-1989-Address.pdf.

6. Champions of Social Justice Who Fought to Protect and Improve Lives

1. Quoted in Patrick Jordan, *Dorothy Day: Love in Action* (Collegeville, MN: Liturgical Press, 2015), 25.

7. Unexpected Trailblazers Who Found Courage to Explore New Paths

1. Quoted in Rubén Cedeño, *Mama Antula* (Buenos Aires: Editorial Metafísica, 2024).

2. John Catoir, *Uplifting Thoughts for Every Day* (Totowa, NJ: Catholic Book Publishing, 2007), 85.

3. Mother Dolores Hart, OSB, and Richard DeNeut, *The Ear of the Heart: An Actress' Journey from Hollywood to Holy Vows* (San Francisco: Ignatius Press, 2013), 34.

4. Hart and DeNeut, *Ear of the Heart*, xi.

5. Hart and DeNeut, *Ear of the Heart*, 62.

6. Hart and DeNeut, *Ear of the Heart*, 202.

7. Hart and DeNeut, *Ear of the Heart*, 224.

8. Hart and DeNeut, *Ear of the Heart*, 233.

9. Hart and DeNeut, *Ear of the Heart*, 406.

10. Hart and DeNeut, *Ear of the Heart*, 425.

8. Compassionate Caregivers: Friends of the Aging, Declining, and Infirm

1. Quoted in Éloi Leclerc, *Song of Silence: The Journey of Saint Jeanne Jugan*, trans. Claire Trocmé (Boston: Daughters of St. Paul, 2009).

2. "About Our Founder," Rosalynn Carter Institute for Caregivers, https://rosalynncarter.org/about-our-founder/.

3. John Paul II, *Evangelium Vitae (On the Value and Inviolability of Human Life)* (March 25, 1995), no. 2, https://www.vatican.va/content/john-paul-ii/en/encyclicals/documents/hf_jp-ii_enc_25031995_evangelium-vitae.html.

4. Quoted in Paul Milcent, *Jeanne Jugan: Humble So as to Love More* (London: Darton, Longman, and Todd, 2000), 15.

5. "Sayings of Jeanne Jugan," Little Sisters of the Poor, https://www.littlesistersofthepoor.co.uk/information/sayings-of-st-jeanne-jugan/.

6. Nourish for Caregivers is an excellent online resource in helping to discern these things: nourishforcaregivers.com.

9. Spiritual Visionaries: Second Act Spirituality Breathes New Life into Old Traditions

1. Quoted in Roberto Zanini, *Bakhita: From Slave to Saint*, trans. Andrew Matt (San Francisco: Ignatius Press, 2013), 81.

2. Maria Morera Johnson, *Our Lady of Charity: How a Cuban Devotion to Mary Helped Me Grow in Faith and Love* (Notre Dame, IN: Ave Maria Press, 2019).

3. Quoted in Alejandro Bermudez, "7 Things You Need to Know about St. Faustina and Her Vision of Hell," Catholic News Agency, October 5, 2023, https://www.catholicnewsagency.com/news/249183/7-things-you-need-to-know-about-st-faustina-and-her-vision-of-hell.

4. "Mary Faustina Kowalska, 1905–1938," Vatican website, https://www.vatican.va/news_services/liturgy/saints/ns_lit_doc_20000430_faustina_en.html.

5. Maria Faustina Kowalska, *Diary: Divine Mercy in My Soul* (Stockbridge, MA: Marians of the Immaculate Conception, 1987), 1588.

6. Quoted in Zanini, *Bakhita*, 60–61.

7. Quoted in Matthew Santucci, "Pope Francis Highlights St. Josephine Bakhita's Example of Forgiveness," Catholic News Agency, October 11, 2023, https://www.catholicnewsagency.com/news/255647/pope-francis-st-josephine-bakhita-forgiveness.

10. Inspired Mentors: Because It's Never Too Late to Be a Badass

1. Elizabeth of the Trinity, "Let Yourself Be Loved," in *Complete Works*, trans. Sister Aletheia Kane, vol. 1, *I Have Found God* (Washington, DC: ICS Publications, 1984), 179.

2. Scott Alessi, "An Icon of Faith, Service, and Basketball," Loyola University Chicago, https://www.luc.edu/sisterjean/.

3. Quoted in Anthony Lilles, "Elizabeth of the Trinity: A Saint for Our Time," *National Catholic Register*, October 16, 2016, https://www.ncregister.com/features/elizabeth-of-the-trinity-a -saint-for-our-time.

4. Quoted in Billy Swan, "St. Elizabeth of the Trinity and Letting Ourselves Be Loved," Word on Fire, November 8, 2023, https://www.wordonfire.org/articles/st-elizabeth-of-the-trinity-and -letting-ourselves-be-loved/.

5. Quoted in Carl Bunderson, "Who Was Elizabeth of the Trinity? The Story Behind a New Saint," Catholic News Agency, June 21, 2016, https://www.catholicnewsagency.com/news/33532/ who-was-elizabeth-of-the-trinity-the-story-behind-a-new-saint.

Maria Morera Johnson is the media editor at Catholicmom.com and author of the award-winning books *My Badass Book of Saints*, *Super Girls and Halos*, and *Our Lady of Charity*. She also contributed to *The Catholic Mom's Prayer Companion*, *Word by Word: Slowing Down with the Hail Mary*, and *Gaze Upon Jesus*. In 2016, Johnson retired from her role as a professor of composition and literature.

Johnson speaks at a number of events, retreats, and conferences, including the National Council of Catholic Women, Austin Women's Conference, and the Catholic Press Association. She's also been featured on CatholicTV and Busted Halo as well as in *Catholic Digest* and *St. Anthony Messenger*.

Johnson is a native of Cuba. She and her husband, John, have three grown children and live in northern Virginia.

mariamjohnson.com
Facebook: @mariajohnson33
X: @bego
Instagram: @begojohnson

ALSO BY MARIA MOREA JOHNSON

My Badass Book of Saints
Courageous Women Who Showed Me How to Live

In this bestseller, Maria Morera Johnson explores the qualities
of twenty-four remarkable and holy women who lived lives of virtue
in unexpected and often difficult circumstances.

Our Lady of Charity
How a Cuban Devotion to Mary Helped Me
Grow in Faith and Love

Maria Morera Johnson shares her childhood memories and heartfelt
stories about devotion to the patroness of Cuba. Journey with her
as she explores how Our Lady of Charity deepened her faith
and guided her to Jesus, offering readers a chance to discover Mary
in a new light and to grow in love and faith.

Super Girls and Halos
My Companions on the Quest for Truth,
Justice, and Heroic Virtue

Super Girls and Halos offers a unique and daring exploration
of the cardinal virtues through the saints and heroines of science
fiction, fantasy, and comic books.